GOD CAN

*Redemption and Hope in
the Drug Abuse War*

Kevin Dennis

PRESS

Rebecca,

God bless you sis as you
take this journey with us! We
love you!

Kevin Dew

"God's a safe-house for the battered,
a sanctuary during bad times.
The moment you arrive, you relax;
you're never sorry you knocked."
Psalms 9:9,10 (MSG)

Table of Contents

Forward

Heroin addiction and drug abuse are a pandemic problem. Children are dying and lives are being cut short. Man lost the war on drugs years ago. Prisons and jails are operating at full capacity due to mostly drug related offenses. My way out of this hell on earth like many others came because of a personal relationship with Jesus Christ.

In 2008 I accepted Jesus as my Lord and Savior. Prior to this life-changing revelation that God was real and that He loved me, there was a huge void in my life. I tried to fill it with things that the world had to offer and failed. How is it possible that a man, with what seemed to be God-given talents and achievements, sink into the depths of darkness and despair and lose all hope for life?

I remember the day a fellow came to me while I was living in a cardboard box in skid row in Los Angeles and asked me this question: "How's it working out for you?" He was referring to the absence of God in my life and having no personal relationship with Jesus Christ. Years of drug and alcohol abuse along with heroin addiction and homelessness had taken its toll on me; I was a broken man. There is one thing that my story and the testaments of faith in this book have in common: "When there is an earthly brokenness, there is a heavenly openness."

The Word of God says there will be trials and tribulations. These seemingly sorrowful events are sometimes necessary for us to seek out truth and turn back to the ways of God.

Through this relationship with our Creator, purpose and destiny are revealed. God loves us so much that he continually repositions us to a place where a relationship with Him becomes a reality. Hearts open up, transformation happens, lives are restored, purpose is revealed, and a peace occurs that surpasses all understanding.

My repositioning came to harvest sitting in a garbage dumpster hungry, while picking ants off of a piece of pizza that had been thrown away. I cried out to God in complete desperation for some kind of hope. Within two days, a man by the name of Mr. Esperanza purchased me a bus ticket away from the life that was killing me. I found out sometime later that "esperanza" in Spanish means hope. In my wildest dreams, I had no idea of the supernatural love and power that was available to me by simply asking our Creator to step in and make my crooked ways straight. I came to Him like a son goes to his daddy and confessed I could not do it alone any longer.

Real life modern day Bible stories and miracles are still alive and well in today's society. Sometimes in life, there seems to be no way out of complicated circumstances when in walks Jesus. Hope, prayer, faith, and new beginnings manifest and the darkness is replaced with light. Our very own Father in Heaven who created us becomes real, available, and tangible.

I believe in my heart that everyone enjoys a happy ending. The supernatural series of events that takes place in this book and in this family's life is absolutely 100% confirmation that truly GOD CAN!

Bobby Hayden, Jr.
P. S. If this can happen for us, it can happen for anyone!

God Can
A Story of Redemption, Hope, and Grace

Preface

The average age when young people begin to "experiment" with drugs continues to slip. With Amber's generation, it was about fourteen years old. Now it is lower. Drug prevention and mental health providers are now going into the grade schools because that is today's hotbed of drug abuse activity. Did you know that? There are so many things we wish we had known when this dark journey started. Let us help you prepare for the war that could be ahead for you and your family. May the Spirit of God also give you hope through the amazing things He does. He raised a life from the dead to do great things for Him. He saved a property from the bulldozer of the demolition crew to bring light to a community.

As my wife and I traveled the dark road of drug addiction with our adult daughter, we struggled with many things. We are both readers. Why is there not a how-to handbook to deal with the legal, family, and church social interactions and train wrecks that come along with this mess? Is there any hope in all this? We believe the stories you are about to experience will give you some foundational decision-making tools. If you are going through the darkness of drug abuse, they will let you know you are not alone in this struggle, lift the shame that comes with the substance abuse stigma, and most of all, give you hope.

God is changing a community. Our little area of Southeastern Ohio is being rocked with the power of God's transformation. Drug abuse is rampant. The fallout from that abuse is on display nearly every day on the front page of our local newspaper. Does that sound familiar? But there is a glimmer of hope. Some are finding victory over substance abuse and the iron clad hold it had on their lives. They are finding victory through the One who can break the chains of addiction. They are realizing that they cannot break them, but there is someone who can. The AA and NA folks call Him the Higher Power—and indeed he is. Let us introduce you to Him in a fresh way. If you do not know Him like the friend that He is, let us invite you to become His best friend forever.

Come take a journey with us.

CHAPTER 1

The Human Toll of Addiction

Amber wilted to the ground in a lifeless lump in our front yard. She had just gotten out of the black Mitsubishi I had helped her purchase so she could work, go to school, and start a new life. Amber had always been a sharp young lady—like her two sisters who had already graduated from college and were on their way to raising great families and having successful careers—and was actually a semester away from becoming an RN. She had a lot going for her–good looking, athletic, and a basketball college scholarship waiting for her. I remember telling her before the game when she ruptured her ACL as a high school freshman, "Remember, you're the hurter, not the hurtee." Little did we know that the pain medication from the surgery that followed her injury would fuel the addiction that already had a foothold in her life from smoking pot.

Earlier that day, a police officer parked beside her house and told us not to call Amber and warn her. He told us that she would be arriving shortly with a car full of stolen property; then he would be ready for her. By this time in our lives, we had dealt with way too many law enforcement encounters. We knew more about law enforcement, the legal system, attorney fees, and the dark underworld of drug addiction than we had ever planned or wanted to know. Somehow that experience is not on most people's bucket list—it just happens.

Dads and moms are called to be the protectors and nurturers of the family, called to raise their children to be all they can be with the God-given gifts and abilities unique only to them. This was not our idea of how to raise a child in the, "nurture and admonition of the Lord," as so eloquently stated in His Book, Ephesians 6:4 (KJV): "And ye fathers, provoke not your children to wrath, but bring them up in the nurture and admonition of the Lord."

The Amplified version expands on that: "Fathers, do not provoke your children to anger [do not exasperate them to the point of resentment with demands that are trivial or unreasonable or humiliating or abusive; nor by showing favoritism or indifference to any of them], but bring them up [tenderly, with loving kindness] in the discipline and instruction of the Lord."

Would you believe me if I told you that we had plenty of "advice" about how to handle our wayward daughter? Ironically, those with the most advice were not the same ones who offered to pray with us for God's wisdom, protection, and comfort each day.

How is that command for nurturing and accountability carried out with a drug-addicted adult child? I don't know how many times we walked the thin line between grace and accountability, hoping against hope that God would preserve her life and give her the strength to turn it around. So we trudged through the college of dealing with drug addiction, and the professors were brutal.

Just as the police officer predicted, the black Mitsubishi pulled up in the driveway, and we, her mom and dad, were there to meet her. Amber tried to cover at first, but we told her that a sheriff's deputy was on the way. Oh yes, she knew something was up. So the handful of pills—only God knows how many and what they were—went into her mouth and down the hatch. She didn't want possession to be added to her charges, and she didn't want anyone to know any more about the enormous black elephant in the room: the specter of drug addiction!

The sheriff deputy pulled up in the driveway that went from her house to ours, and as soon as he got out of his car he taped Amber's car doors shut to preserve the evidence. Then he tried to question the offender to get all the information he could for a solid conviction, and possibly leads that would result in returning the stolen property to its rightful owners. When Amber fell in a motionless heap there in our front yard, the officer believed she was faking it to get out of talking. He didn't waste any time letting all of us know that either. Little did any of us realize, she was just a few precious breaths away from death.

The 911 emergency techs had seen this all too often. Nobody wants to hear those words: drug overdose. Contrary to the perception of many folks, intentional overdose rarely happens. Usually the addict's judgment is so impaired that some crazy event triggers them to take too many pills. Or enter King Heroin, the drug of choice today. The mix of the drug provided by the sellers, who themselves are likely addicts, is inconsistent at best. Hey, look at the mentality, or lack thereof, of the "cooks." Today's heroin is often mixed with Fentanyl, which is ten times more potent than straight heroin. Fentanyl can be found in pain patches, and too much of it will kill you as it enters your blood system from a nasty used or clean exchanged needle— it doesn't matter. Death doesn't sweat the small stuff. Some people rub it like snuff between their lip and gum.

Amber would survive that hospital stay, black carbon poison antidote, stomach pump, and the lifesaving dedication of the local hospital emergency room workers. Then the legal proceedings and sentencing remained. Again. But thank you, Jesus—we have stood by dear friends who would have loved to be standing beside a hospital bed. Instead they stood by a coffin of one whose life ended way too early. May God be with those caught up in substance abuse and with their precious families. The dads and moms, grandparents and siblings, in-laws, cousins, aunts and uncles, and loved ones of all kinds struggle to walk that line between accountability and grace, praying that the lifesaving safety net they are weaving will be enough.

CHAPTER **2**

Desperation Births Hope

"W hat do you see?" The elder senior pastor watched and wondered as his protégée, a young associate pastor, peered out his office window at the dilapidated building. The old school building sat on a parcel of forty-six acres across the state route that divided the church property from the former school property. Scrub bushes, trees, and tall weeds nearly hid the building from view. The old flat roof, the subject of many school board meetings I am sure, was falling in—pieces of it were strewn about the ground around the school. We would find out later that it had been replaced several times—several layers of old rubber, asphalt, and about any kind of roofing you can imagine. As it fell, it brought piles of asbestos-laden roofing material that had been sprayed onto the ceiling with it. Asbestos was a great building material at one time, before its deadly respiratory effects were widely known.

The year was 2008. The specter of drug abuse was well known but not well understood, at least not in our little circle. But we did have something that the Spirit of God had given us through divine inspiration and the leadership of our pastors—a heart for those who were often thrown on the scrapheap of humanity. Yes—they had broken into homes and stolen peoples' precious possessions, starting with their families. Yes—they

had burned many relationship bridges. Yes—they had manip-
ulated even seniors and grandparents to get money to feed the
monster, and the monster's appetite grew with each feeding. A
nuisance to society, lock them up, reward their poor decision
making, and kill them if you get a chance. Gun ownership does
indeed increase when people feel threatened.

In Matthew 25, Jesus is giving the disciples a hint about
how the final judgment will be carried out. He told about a king
who was passing out His inheritance to a blessed new world
and who got to enter this wonderful world. Helping the "least of
these" was one of the criteria. The king will answer, "Whenever
you did it for any of my people, no matter how unimportant
they seemed, you did it for me" (CEV). The Message puts it
another way: "Then those 'sheep' are going to say, 'Master,
what are you talking about? When did we ever see you hungry
and feed you, thirsty and give you a drink? And when did we
ever see you sick or in prison and come to you?' Then the King
will say, 'I'm telling the solemn truth: Whenever you did one
of these things to someone overlooked or ignored, that was
me—you did it to me." Is there anyone more "least" than the
drug addicted? Is there anyone in our society who is looked
down upon more? OK, in 2016 we might point to others like
the burgeoning homeless population, but you get the picture in
vivid HD color—the drug addicted are among them. Especially
the sick and in prison—you will see.

Enter Gallia Strong Tower. Beginning around 2004 in Vinton
Baptist Church, a small group of parents with addicted children
and others who had a heart to see God's healing in their lives
made a bold move. They started meeting with those who would
come in small groups, talked about drug addiction, and prayed
for victory over it. The parents and loved ones of those caught
up in drug addiction needed the love and support of each other.
The shame and guilt of drug addiction is a heavy load for the
addict, but the parents and loved ones bear it as well. Where
did I go wrong? What can I do now? Rehab, counseling, a psy-
chologist, a psychiatrist? All the options are complicated by an
adult addicted to drugs—they really don't have to do anything

until they enter the legal or law enforcement system. And that system is not designed to meet the needs of drug addicts—just to do the best job they can of protecting society!

In 2006, Gallia Strong Tower was born; bylaws were written, and steps were taken to make it a formal organization. GST would be its own organization but closely associated with the church. We had learned by now that this recovery thing was hopeless without help that came from outside of our little circle. Hey, isn't that Step 1 in the tried-and-true Recovery process? Starting with Alcoholics Anonymous, then Narcotics Anonymous, and now the Celebrate Recovery program, based on the eight Biblical Beatitudes, Step 1 is "We admitted we were powerless over our addictions and compulsive behaviors, that our lives had become unmanageable." As leaders of a new outreach, we knew something else that was closely related: we did not have the collective wisdom to defeat the monster without a higher power. Step 2—"We came to believe that a power greater than ourselves could restore us to sanity."

So what actually works? Like so many of life's great moments of understanding, the key is before us and obvious if our spirit is in tune with His. He is waiting to give us the key when we are ready to receive it. Life change can happen. It has for many. Sometimes it happens in a moment of time—a life changing decision that allows the Spirit of God to radically change a person's thinking and actions. More often than not, it does not happen that way. Recovery is hard work. I have often drawn a graph for our new folks who come into the Recovery outreach. It looks something like this—a timeline of doing well in recovery and relapsing into addiction. The starting point is this. That person whose life is ruled by how to get the next fix, high, pill, or syringe of their drug of choice exercises the beautiful free will instilled in them when they were created by the Spirit of God. They call on that higher power and others around them who love them and ask for help.

TIME

We were exiting a church service where a recovered addict had given a powerful testimony about the instant life change God had performed in him—turned his life of drug addiction and hell into one of joy and service for the One who changed him. My senior pastor was shaking his head as we opened the back doors of the worship area and prepared to greet those who would leave the service. "What's the matter? I asked. Wasn't that one of the most powerful stories of life change you have ever heard?"

"I am thinking of all those who heard the message and are struggling—who will never have an experience like that. I wonder what is in their hearts right now." What wisdom, and what a reminder that we are in this recovery thing for the long haul!

There is a rehab program that has an independently verified 87 percent success rate of recovered addicts, based on their lives seven years later. That program, Teen Challenge, has many recovery sites across the country. Teen Challenge recognizes that a faith-based and long-term recovery is the key. Yes, we do trust in a higher power. And He has a name. His name is Jesus, and He can change you from the inside out!

I bet you are wondering what happened to that old, dilapidated building. Stay tuned.

CHAPTER 3

Can't Happen

The knock on the door came late at night—not usually a good sign when you are struggling with an adult child who has an addiction. I knew the young sheriff's deputy well. "Hey, have you ever seen a safe float?"

My reply: "I'm not sure that can happen. Safes are strong and heavy, but I don't know that they are water-tight." The deputy agreed. They don't float. But this one did.

"I was just driving around chasing leads on the latest robbery and passed the pond down below your house. I just happened to look over at the pond, and a safe was floating on top the water. It was the same one that was stolen from the church. We're pretty sure your daughter was in on that one. The sheriff's office wants to talk to her. She can come in, or we can come pick her up. It would be better for her if she came on her own."

Now one thing you, and your wife in my case, become when you go through this life-rending experience is a quasi-lawyer. OK—I try and talk her into going to the sheriff's office. Would it really be better for her? One thing we learned early on is that for whatever reason, verbal promises made by law enforcement folks will not always be kept. Maybe the courts enter the picture and things change, superiors tell officers that the promises cannot be kept, the officer is trying to talk you into what is best, there could be manipulation going on that leads to a faster conviction with less work. Take your pick. Throw a dart. Suffice it to say that you will live the truth of the famous sculpture of lady justice holding the scales and wearing a blindfold. Justice is not only blind but often unfair in the eyes of those dealing with the fallout of broken laws and broken lives.

So how do you navigate those waters? Where is the rule book? Here is the bad news: there ain't one, hasn't been written yet, not on the bestsellers list. So how do you deal with all that? Oh, there is no lack of advice. There will be many who have the answers—they run the gamut from your severely lacking parental skills to what is wrong with the country at large—drug addicts on the loose, terrorizing the neighborhood. I am not minimizing that. My heart aches for those who have been abused by the abusers—thefts, broken windows and doors, precious and unreplaceable heirloom jewelry or guns that have been stolen, the list goes on. You cannot know the violated and unsettled feeling of having your home, your safe castle, broken into and being ransacked, until you actually experience it.

I'm sure there are many avenues of coping, but here are the three that my wife and I considered and/or saw played out in the lives of our daughter and others who were dealing with adult loved ones who had addictions.

Strategy #1: Keep them out of prison at any cost. County jails are often a nasty and abusive environment. You are locked up with violent members of society who are often detoxing from drug abuse. Detox is brutal. The details are not nice; it has been compared to having the flu, only about ten times worse. You get the picture. Prisons have their own issues. State prisons share a common problem with county jails— society in general is not interested in funding to make them livable. "They deserve to be there. That's why they call it jail." Yep, I've heard those words many times. I want to say right now that I am not slamming those who oversee and actually work in these facilities. Some are not good people, but many are. Those who have been incarcerated will tell you of acts of kindness or encouragement by some of the guards or other front-line folks. God bless them. They are dealing with a lot too—trying to do a job that is typically way underfunded and way underappreciated.

So hire a great lawyer with a reputation for getting people off scot-free. I hope you have a hefty bank account or sufficient equity to take out a large loan. The good ones, not even the great ones, may charge by the hour. Two hundred dollars an hour or more would not be unusual, and a fifteen-minute minimum means if you call to ask how the weather is, you can expect a bill for fifty dollars. Oh, and if you don't pay the bill on time—all you have invested is gone. Here are the pitfalls. Unless your loved one is ready to quit, you are flushing money down the drain. Then there is the risk of putting them back on the street—using, stealing, and a prime candidate for accidental overdose or being shot while breaking into a home. The third drawback is that the addict may not experience true accountability and repentance. Listen, there is no script. I have actually seen this appear to work. I have also seen it end in tragedy. I have no criticism for those who try—I have only prayers from one who has been there. In the state of Ohio, where I live, accidental overdose has overtaken vehicle accidents for the past four years running as the number one killer in the state. This strategy gets an "A" for grace but not so much for accountability.

Strategy #2: Turn 'em loose. Sink or swim. You made your own bed, now lay in it. Tough love. I once had a lady ask me, when our daughter was in state prison for the second time, "Have you ever considered tough love?" I knew enough about her family life that I could have burnt her to the ground. God calls us to walk the high road, so I smiled and asked for her prayers. If an adult addict has family members who care about them, a couple of things may happen. The addict may burn bridges so severely with thefts, public embarrassment, physical or verbal fights, and other byproducts of addiction that the loved ones are finished. Or the loved ones may have had all their resources stolen or used in legal fees that they could have used to help the addicted.

The main problem with this strategy is that a person with an active addiction is not thinking clearly. Depending on the time spent in the throes of addiction, the type of chemicals used, and other factors such as their individual tolerance, the brain of the addicted is physiologically damaged, and critical thinking is short circuited. Now we turn that person loose to make life decisions with the advice of a public defender. Public defenders are lawyers assigned by the state when the defendant cannot afford one, typically the case for an adult addict. Some of them may be very good lawyers, but the case load often prevents them from spending the time on a case that is necessary. Your chances of a great outcome in the courtroom just took a nosedive. This strategy gets an "A" for accountability but not so much for grace.

Strategy #3: Mix accountability with grace. Walk the tightrope. Try and make a safety net to keep them alive, yet allow them to feel the pain of drug abuse and its fallout so they will hopefully come to their senses. We learned some "tricks of the trade." If the addict says they need food, get them a bag—don't give them money. Cash is a trigger. No matter what their intent, when they see it, it will likely go for the next hit of _____. Fill in the blank for your loved one. There are lots of creative things you can do with GPS trackers that do not cost a lot of money. Our daughter lived behind our house, so monitoring was easier at times. I have run drug dealers off my property, sometimes in ways that I am not proud to remember. Thank you, Jesus, for your protection.

We turned Amber over to the public defenders but tried to work with them. They are overworked and appreciate your doing some of the leg work within the constraints of legal protocol. My wife became a detective extraordinaire. Not that I want to break the law, but if I did, she would nail me in a heartbeat. We sacrificed to keep Amber in her own house. That had its pitfalls, but we did not have to worry as much about our own well-being—account information or other sensitive information being compromised, worrying every time we left the house, and so on. Get an alarm system. It is not expensive compared to the cost if you don't. The only time we hired a lawyer was to get temporary custody of Amber's only daughter and our granddaughter. Thank you, Jesus for allowing us to have that custody and give her a somewhat normal childhood. She is today a great kid with a heart for God and loves her mom. This strategy seemed to be a great balance of accountability and grace.

CHAPTER 4

The X Factor

"I have some good news for you, and I have some bad news for you." The young associate pastor who had caught the vision was talking to the owners of the old North Gallia High School property. "The good news is that Vinton Baptist wants this property. But … the problem is that we don't have any money." Subduing laughter I am sure, the owner said they would like to donate the property but couldn't do that because they had too much invested. They had planned to change the property into a church camp.

"I was on vacation, and God woke me up at three o'clock in the morning. He told me that we will own the property across the road—the old North Gallia High School." The new VBC senior pastor was on a roll. Father time had changed the former senior pastor's position on the staff, and a new leader was preaching. As chairman of the Finance Board who was painfully aware of our paltry church operating fund, I thought, "Good luck with that. God will have to do it, because we sure can't!"

About three weeks later, I got one of those calls that is a landmark in the birth of a movement. "Call this person with the full amount, and they will send you a check for the North Gallia property." When the fog began to clear about what was happening, I realized that the total would be the $100,000 property cost, closing costs, and so on "Just call with the total amount. They will send you a check." Enter the X Factor. When there is no other way it is going to happen or even possible, the Spirit of God shows up and moves a mountain. He is at work in ways we cannot see. A family familiar with the ravages of substance abuse on young lives had stepped up to make the impossible possible. Thank you, family with a heart for others. Thank you, Jesus. Hope had been conceived, and now the embryo was growing.

Here's the deal. Most investors feared the property because the number tossed around was a cool million to clean all the asbestos from the old building. Sure, there was lots of space and the largest gym in the county. Sure, there was a state-of-the-art sewage treatment plant ready to be fired up after the vandal damage was repaired. But a million bucks? How will that work? You guessed it—the X Factor. In my former work with a major Midwest utility, I knew something about asbestos removal. Most of the contaminated material was in the plaster covering the ceiling throughout the building. And most of the plaster was piled on the floor. The old flat roof had suffered major failure, and years of neglect and rainfall had soaked up the ceiling plaster while father gravity did the rest! You could barely walk through the building for the piles of plaster and other debris. One of our first tasks was to barricade the building for safety.

A term used to make asbestos safe to handle, so that its deadly fibers are not released into the air, is "adequately wet." And boy was it! The water ran out of the piles of debris onto the floor of the old building. God was laying out a plan. In our state there was a rule that allowed removal of that kind of debris by non-licensed workers. Pipe insulation, ceiling material, and so on had to be removed by a licensed contractor. I ran a procedure past the state health department folks, an approved asbestos landfill that would take the material, and some of the experts at my former company. The plan would work. It was legal and protected our volunteers well beyond the requirements of the law.

We just "happened to have"—enter the X Factor—a member of the congregation who was trained to teach asbestos removal safety and to make sure workers could properly wear a respirator. A properly worn and engineered respirator is the last line of defense that would keep any airborne fibers from entering a person's delicate respiratory system. Our industry friends provided respirators, white work suits, hard hats, and gloves to do the work at no cost to us. About thirty volunteers were trained in the work, and their protection went way beyond what was actually required. But that building was going to be used by God to rebuild and protect precious lives. Why not start in the beginning? Have you ever sweat, bled, and worked to exhaustion with a group of people who cared deeply about the work and had a common heart to see it done? That bond will last for eternity. That bond is a blessing on earth that cannot be duplicated. It is reserved for a special time in a special place with a special blend of people. Maybe that is what the verse in Proverbs 17:17 is talking about: "A friend loves at all times, and a brother is born for a time of adversity" (NIV).

So picture this if you can. A group of men suit up in their white Tyvek zip-up work suits. Then they don their respirators, hard hats, and other gear. The first and most important part of the day has already happened. The forty-cup coffee pot has been a popular gathering place. Breakfast might include the area's famous Amish donuts—fresh, soft, and sweet glazed donuts that would overflow the normal donut plate for sure. When you work like we did, you actually did burn off all those calories and more! And now the kicker—the main course, the secret to success. So sacred a duty—dare we even discuss it. Invite the X Factor. As this makeshift work crew began each day, they joined hands and asked the Spirit of God to be in the work and to protect each worker. Let's see—no serious injuries, zero labor disputes, an amazing time of comradery—thank you, Jesus, for working among us. You were the unseen hand who directed our work and protected us from harm.

Several weekends and large waste hoppers later, the work was done. You could actually walk through the building. The plies of broken concrete blocks, wood, and other construction debris went out with the ceiling waste because it was all in the same contaminated junk pile. Now came another landmark. The EPA has a program that provides grants for cleaning up asbestos in order to reuse a building. They are highly competitive. In 2012 an application was sent to the EPA for $200,000 to remove the remainder of the asbestos on the ceiling, pipes, floor tile, and anywhere else the inspectors might find it. The application was from a church, since VBC owned the property. The grant application was a ton of work. Since we didn't have the money to hire a professional grant writer, it was largely written by me with input from other FOH folks, guidance from EPA contacts, and a lot of prayer. The final draft was laid on the church alter, and we prayed over it before its submission. For an old power company guy, this relationship with the EPA was refreshing—not having to negotiate permits and so on, but working with them to get much needed help. The state and federal folks were a great bunch to work with!

But a church represented by a rag-tag collection of folks not familiar with the detailed and complicated grant process? Really? What did we have going for us? A vision, a heart to work, a great reputation with our partners at all levels of our community, and—drum roll, please—the X Factor.

CHAPTER 5

No Respecter

C ome on in to my office, and let's talk about Amber. We had reached the end of what we knew to do. Discipline, threats, removing privileges, using every parenting skill we had learned while raising three beautiful girls did not seem to work. By now her oldest sister was away from home, living with her new husband in Louisiana. Her other older sister was going to college and soon to be married. Both of them were beginning to build what would be great lives and great families. While we parents saw that as the blessing of God, Amber saw it in another way—she was falling short. Why can't I get there? What is wrong with me? The harder she tried to be "normal," the louder the dark specter of drug addiction called her name and invited her to cope with life the quick and easy way.

Her substance abuse continued to worsen after the ACL surgery from a basketball injury at fourteen years old. But we were only able to catch glimpses into that world. Is she really doing that? You cannot believe the power of denial until you experience it as a parent and look back. Nobody wants to believe that their child is "one of those people." I raised them right. I prayed for them. I turned the book of Proverbs inside out, asking God to help me parent this child. I memorized and trusted Proverbs 22:6: "Train up a child in the way he should go: and when he is old, he will not depart from it" (KJV). The NIV says it this way: "Start children off on the way they should go, and even when they are old they will not turn from it." So what's up with that? We did that. We know there are no perfect parents, but we followed the admonition of the Book that God wrote as best we could with the help of the Holy Spirit.

By the way, I have a new appreciation for the phrase "When he/she is old." There was a time in my life when I believed that proper training for a child resulted in a fool-proof mature teenager. Oh yes, that's when my children were young. Now I have a new take on that age range. When our adult children "get it" and return to the foundational teaching they received as youths, that is the time I believe the Proverbs passage references. But what if some never get it and leave this earth without returning to the God of their youth? The death of an unrepentant person is heartbreaking. Their soul's destiny is a locked agreement between them and their Creator that nobody else can really see. And I know this about training—it takes a willing trainer and a willing trainee. You can lead an athlete to the weight room, but you can't make them excel if they do not have the heart for it. It is the same when receiving any sound training.

You know, there are life moments when the light comes on. You know it is time for a change, and you get the courage to do it. We are not going to lose this battle, and the dark one is not going to claim another young life—at least not until we have fought with all that we have. There are no givens in the war—only the casualties of drug addiction that end in death, imprisonment, and lives broken physically and emotionally. Thank God some have a miraculous turning point in their lives, often when they acknowledge the One who created them and gave His life for them.

So the moment when life changed and we came out of denial arrived when we found pot in Amber's suitcase. We were packing for a family vacation to our favorite destination—Myrtle Beach. We had reluctantly, and after Amber's incessant pleading, allowed her to take a friend. We didn't want her to have a cohort in crime but were thinking about the possibility of true R&R for ourselves by having someone to help keep her busy. Then we discovered the pot. Oh, it wasn't hers. You will hear that a lot. Just like the cigarettes and lighters from a much earlier incident—they belonged to a friend. Then denial kicks in. The story is almost believable because they can be so convincing. But not this time. We drove a stake in the ground—it is time for all-out war in the battle for our daughter's life. Call your friend—the deal is off. Wow, did the battle ever ensue! It was a far from perfect vacation, but we did get some relaxation among the battles and further realization of where our daughter was.

I could tell you some scary stories about events of that time away but will only share one. As we were catching on to the secret lifestyle Amber had been living, we began looking for signs. We had come into the full-blown cell phone era, and we made sure the kids had one if we were separated, especially in a place like a beach resort town. Amber had gone out and not returned. She didn't answer her phone. After a while we launched a search and rescue—not knowing if she had been harmed or was just being her rebellious self. We were staying in a family resort along the beach with several multi-level accommodations that had elevators. We found her in one of those, sitting on the floor, messed up. So much for the family resort. It wasn't their fault. The dark one can find you anywhere if you have the heart to look for him. He is no respecter of people or places. In fact, he will look for you. I Peter 5:8 says he is "like a roaring lion. He prowls around looking for someone to swallow up" (NIRV).

"OK, I have some thoughts for you," the clinical psychiatrist continued. "Do you think that your strict parenting might contribute to Amber's rebellion?"

What a breath of fresh air! Halleluiah! Here all of our "friends" and homemade psychiatrists told us we were too easy on her!

She continued. "And dad, do you think that all of that hard discipline might be causing Amber to rebel and even turn to drugs to cope with all that?"

Wait a minute! Hold your horses! My wife and I looked at each other. The light went on again. Score another one for

Amber. Nothing sticks. Just when you think you have the goods on them and this will do the trick, the tables are spun. OK, we are *supposed to feel guilty*—for what? Trying to save a life? Trying to keep a young girl out of jail? Loving a child enough to be tough when needed?

So let me introduce you to a psychological phenomenon that those in the drug world have perfected. Manipulation. You have never experienced it like you are about to if you are going to deal with a person in full-blown drug addiction. Oh I know—you thought the salesman ripped you off because you listened to his well-polished presentation when he talked you into spending more money than you knew you should. You thought he got one over on you. Or the outreach leader who tugged on your heart and talked you into volunteering more time than you had to volunteer. How did he talk me into that? I still can't quite figure it out. Well, fasten your seatbelt. Grab your saddle horn, because you are about to go on the ride of your life on a bucking bronco that means business.

Here's the deal. We have to understand that once addiction kicks in, it trains an addict's mind and body to feel that there is only one truly important thing in life—where and how do I get my next high? In her book *Power Over Addiction*, Dr. Mary Holley illustrates the physiological changes that occur in the addict's brain as addiction progresses. They seem to be a different person because they are becoming a different person. The addict's body, brain, and emotions are all directed at obtaining that next high. The high could originate from a number of sources, which are referred to in the recovery world as the "drug of choice." These drugs have included alcohol, prescription pills or pain patches, marijuana in its many forms, inhalants, hallucinogens, methamphetamines, cocaine, king heroin, and many variations of the aforementioned substances.

Heroin has become king in many parts of our country because of its relatively low cost and high availability. OxyContin is a timed-release pain killer and used to be the king in our area. At the peak of its abuse, an 80 mg pill could sell for over $100, and someone highly addicted could take six to eight in one day. Reformulation of the pill plus efforts by law enforcement, the courts, and the medical profession have all worked to make medications like OxyContin harder for the addict to obtain and use. On the other hand, due to a high influx of heroin into our country, a single "hit" can be purchased for $10 or less. Of course, as the addiction rises, so does the amount and cost of the drug. The addict continues to pay this rising price as they chase that original high. The original high cannot be repeated, and soon an addict needs a certain amount just to feel "normal" and not suffer the living hell of withdrawal.

The addict becomes an expert liar and manipulator to get the funds required to support his/her habit. You are looking at your adult loved one, trying to reason with them, and using every persuasive argument you can conceive. You desperately want them to be healed of their drug addiction. They are looking you in the eye, and you think you are making progress. They are really thinking, "What can I say to convince them that I must have $100 cash tonight and that I will pay it back soon?" Or they may be scanning the surroundings to see if there is any prime location for cash that can be easily taken. Legion are the loved ones who have given addicts money, knowing in the back of their minds that it was for drugs. Yet the addict's reasoning was so persuasive. You see, they have a lot on the line. They also have a network of fellow addicts who provide all sorts of ideas and proven con strategies that work. And we love them. Oh how we love them and want to believe that they are getting better.

So the manipulation becomes a honed skill that reaches even beyond the family to medical professionals, mental health providers, and any others who are not aware of the addict's background and the psychological twists they can lay on you. And so we press on, loving, hoping, praying.

CHAPTER **6**

Out of the Fibers

I t was 9:00 AM on Thursday, May 24, 2012, in Ballroom 4 at the Ohio Convention Center in Columbus—the second day of the Ohio Brownfield annual convention. The lead pastor of Vinton Baptist Church and I hoofed it to the convention center from near the AEP headquarters building along the Scioto River, where we had found parking for the day. I knew about the parking area from my old days with AEP. My pastor was the one who believed he had heard from God about the property across the road, and the funds to purchase had appeared a short time later. Then he mentioned the Brownfield opportunity. I knew about the program from my working days in the environmental field but never really connected it with cleaning up the old school property until our pastor brought it up.

We thought the X Factor was once again at work with the Brownfield grant opportunity. When I discussed it with a former AEP colleague, he invited me and the VBC pastor to stay overnight the evening before the Thursday meeting. We had a wonderful time of a meal together and the genuine fellowship that is a powerful time for brothers in Christ. Our host and I are both connoisseurs of fine Cajun cuisine, and he prepared some gumbo for us that was right out of the Louisiana back country! Wow! This plan just seemed to be falling more and more into place with each confirmation.

A valuable lesson learned through all of this is the truth of Proverbs 11:14 (WEB) "Where there is no wise guidance, the nation falls, but in the multitude of counselors there is victory." As we navigate life's toughest pathways, we do well to remember that there is wisdom in many counselors. The cleanup of the old school was just a microcosm of how God can work through many folks with different backgrounds and gift sets. When they are united with a common goal and are willing to obey the call of God, He can multiply each one's gifts through the collective team to do great things. Better than that, He can do more than we can even ask or think. In fact, Ephesians 3:20 (MSG) says, "God can do anything, you know—far more than you could ever imagine or guess or request in your wildest dreams! He does it not by pushing us around but by working within us, his Spirit deeply and gently within us. Glory to God!"

The Brownfield concept is a program where the federal government provides matching grant funds through the states to perform cleanup of property contaminated with hazardous materials. The grants are highly competitive—a complicated application process must be followed. The application took months of painstaking work, meetings with the state folks, and even learning an electronic organization tool that kept all the information in the right order for you to submit. Whew! The goal of the Brownfield money is to restore property that will eventually have a useful purpose. Typically old contaminated properties present a hazard to the community as well as an eyesore, vandalism site, and a general reduction in property values because of their presence. The Brownfield program seeks to convert the net negatives of a run-down property to a net positive by converting a property for job creation, improved aesthetics, and hopefully to be used in a way that builds up the community and does not detract from it.

Early on the first steps were to have a site review by the state folks. The team who worked with the Field of Hope (FOH) was excellent. They guided us through all the requirements, trained us, and seemed to really have a heart for the work that was both being done and going to be done at the FOH. Teamwork was critical, and I believe that God sent the right people to be a part of the FOH work. It was refreshing and a new experience for me to be on that side of the state and federal environmental folks. In my work with a major utility, I often had to negotiate the fine points of permits, respond to site inspections, and so on that put me on the other side of the environmental folks. But now I was working with great professionals with a common goal to clean up a nasty site and make it usable so it could help build up a community ravaged too long by the effects of substance abuse.

The vision of the FOH has been threefold:

1. Expand the Food Pantry operation currently at the church site. Each year about eight thousand clients are served from around the community, and the church has no space to expand. The expanded Food Pantry could feed more people, allow clothes and appliances to be displayed better, and provide storage for shipment to other area food pantries.
2. Expand the large gymnasium into an operating youth center where young people could learn team sports and get life coaching as well. May God use this to prevent many from entering the clutches of substance abuse.
3. Build a long-term, faith-based residential rehabilitation center where folks can achieve real-life victory over substance abuse. Residential housing would be built, and the main building would be used for life and job skill training. The FOH Counseling Center would also be housed there. Folks in the FOH residential program as well as folks who participated on an outpatient basis would find victory there.

Surely the FOH project filled the bill for a Brownfield cleanup site to a T. When we got to the Convention Center, we realized that a whole host of other folks thought the same thing about their projects. The first day of the conference had been full of great information and contacts regarding Brownfield work. There were a lot of well-dressed and well-spoken folks there from the professional and government worlds. It was apparent that we were fairly small fish in a big pond, or maybe the Pacific Ocean. We did meet some outstanding folks, though, and began building relationships that still last today. We met a number of folks from the state and federal governments—engineers, contractors, and consultants who really believed in what was happening with the property and wanted to help in any way that they could.

And now it was zero hour—crunch time—the time that all grant applicants and the professional folks who might support them were waiting for. The VBC pastor and I were sitting with some of our newfound friends at a round table filled with hot coffee and great conversation. We were sharing past experiences and hopes and dreams for the future. One of the folks asked us, "Who led your grant writing team on the grant submittal?" Well, there's only one word to adequately describe what I felt: *awkward.* I'm usually a pretty quick and confident responder in a conversation but had to scramble a bit to answer that one. "Well, I pretty much wrote it but had a lot of help from other folks supplying information. The E tool that organizes the grant information for you was a great help as well." There was an uneasy silence, like when you give a really crazy comment to a Sunday School lesson in front of the whole class and as soon as you say it, you think, "Oh nuts, did I really say that?" Nobody wants to correct it and embarrass you with the truth.

Finally the silence was broken by one of our newfound and sympathetic friends. Wow, that doesn't usually happen. Have you written grants before? The answer was yes but on a much smaller scale. Isn't that amazing how God works? I had been in a volunteer position with a county chemical emergency response team during my utility working days. One of my jobs was to write grants although on a much, much smaller scale. Anyway, it was a start. But he continued. Most folks have a team of writers with each one contributing their part. Oh, I didn't mention that the grant writing was just one of the many things on my plate. You servants of God working diligently through our beloved local churches know exactly what I am talking about. You wear many hats and pray each day for guidance as you navigate through the work before you. I looked at my pastor as we read between the lines and were in silent agreement—"We ain't got a snowball's chance in the hot place of getting a grant."

There were several high level government folks there for the event. As much as I have been a critic at times of our government, I want to go on record as saying for that particular day, we met some great and dedicated public servants. A number of folks gave talks about rebuilding our communities and the many lives that our communities impact as well. I was especially impressed with a young man who was introduced as a member of the President's cabinet. He quoted from Proverbs during his passionate talk—a strong believer in Christ, unless I am missing the mark. I chased him down after his talk as he hustled off to get to his next duty and thanked him for his boldness with the scripture. What a blessing—His followers are in all walks of life, I believe! But now it was zero hour. Thoughts were buzzing through my head. I remembered laying the stack of paper that was the completed grant request on the altar of my church and folks gathering around praying for its success. We believed together that it would fuel the hope of a community. We believed together that the only force that could defeat the specter of drug addiction was the power of God through His greater church—the community of believers in our area. Was God really in this mess? Lord, give us grace no matter what.

Mathy Stanislaus, Assistant Administrator, U.S. EPA, took the stage. We all knew the implications of the next few minutes. A lot of hard work, and financial investment for many of the groups, was on the line. Seven grant awards would be made for the great state of Ohio for the year 2012. The speaker made some initial comments and then came to the "time we had all been waiting for." As he began to read down the list of award winners, we recognized that Ohio's cities and metropolitan areas would get the funding. That makes sense I suppose—a great need we were sure and a team of professionals to support a project. As the speaker read off the grant number six award winner, my pastor and I locked eyes, and we could read each other's thoughts—ain't happening today. Mr. Stanislaus continued: "—and Number Seven is $200,000 to Vinton Baptist Church from Vinton, Ohio." *Wow.* Praise God! Our entire table erupted in applause, hand shaking, and the look of witnessing an epic David versus Goliath struggle. We were completely overwhelmed in the moment, and my only wish was that my wife and the team who had labored so faithfully on the project could have been there to share in the victory. Our friends at the table were surprised as well but elated to be part of the miracle—they were genuinely happy for the project! It was a surreal moment. You live and work, hope and pray, then God shows up and gives you a mountain top experience. He had defied the odds. He made the seemingly impossible possible. When all else failed, the X Factor claimed the day!

CHAPTER 7

Assorted Bottoms

The young man smiled at me and said, "You know, prison isn't always the worst thing that can happen." My wife and I were not prepared to receive that. Our young Recovery outreach was just getting started in 2006, and we were benchmarking—learning how others did the work—at other rehabilitation facilities. We had traveled from our location to Piketon, Ohio, where a lady who had done prison time was starting a rehabilitation outreach. Her husband was the pastor of a nearby church which worked closely with the clients in recovery. There were a number of young men living in a recovery house, working through the faith-based twelve-step program, and receiving training to be assimilated back into "normal" life. Here's how I could best describe the lady who started the outreach: fearless, energetic, spirit-filled, creative, resourceful, and having a huge heart for those caught up in substance abuse.

They had two weekly meetings. One was just for the clients, and the second was open to the public—prospective outreach workers like us, family members looking for answers, also some of us, and the general public who want to learn more about substance abuse. They brought in a few guys to tell their story of addiction and how they were trying to get victory over it. We learned two truths that quite honestly I doubted at the time. But they proved to be true in Amber's life and the life of many others who have passed through our outreach.

The first truth I am talking about has a lesson named for it in the "Celebrate Recovery" twelve-step lesson series that we use in our Recovery outreach, Gallia Strong Tower. Lesson 21 is "Relapse." I hate that lesson. I hate the truth of that lesson. I hate the pain to the addict and their family/friends when relapse is lived out. You get the picture. I don't really hate the lesson because we need to realize the truth of it, but I just hate the resulting distrust that re-enters a relationship, broken promises, jail time, the pain, and all the rest. And most of all, I hate it for the addict who now feels like a piece of human crap. How could I do that to those I love? Why am I so weak? Why is there no hope for me when others can get it? You get the picture.

When you really search your heart about this whole addiction thing, you realize that there is a lot of hypocrisy on the part of us who are "clean." Now follow closely. There are many passages of scripture we could use, but let's go to 1 John 1:8–10. The book of 1 John was written to the New Testament church—a circular letter to be sent to several churches to help ensure they were grounded in the right doctrine of Christ for the age of grace. This passage says (MSG) "If we claim that we're free of sin, we're only fooling ourselves. A claim like that is errant nonsense. On the other hand, if we admit our sins— make a clean breast of them—he won't let us down; he'll be true to himself. He'll forgive our sins and purge us of all wrongdoing. If we claim that we've never sinned, we out-and-out contradict God—make a liar out of him. A claim like that only shows off our ignorance of God." Remember that was written to the New Testament churches—believers. When we as believers give in to this earthly body and sin, we will find ready forgiveness when we genuinely repent.

Here's another way of looking at it. We're a child of the King, doing pretty good. Then wham! That old sinful nature gets us again. Sin. Call it relapse in the area of _____. You fill it in. There's one huge difference when we relapse and when the addict relapses. Depending on the nature of our relapse, very few people or maybe nobody at all except for us and God know about it. The addict usually isn't so lucky. When he relapses, the results of that misstep often cannot be hidden. Here are some ways that relapse into drug abuse shows its ugly self:

- Alienation of family and friends who recognize someone claiming to be clean is obviously high
- Failing a drug test if the addict is in a legal or treatment program that requires testing
- Arrest or charges by law enforcement due to driving while impaired, stealing to get money for drugs, physical violence from a bad drug deal in the dark world of drug trafficking, and so on.
- Discovery may result in violating probation and sending the addict back to prison or jail.
- Self-confession by the addict because they are overwhelmed with guilt.
- The dark feeling described by Amber as "being at the bottom of a long, dark hole and not being able to see the top."

So when is enough enough? When is it time to call off the craziness, get off drugs, and get healing? That is not a simple question. I have never experienced the hell of withdrawal. The fear of experiencing that drives many who are addicted to keep snorting, shooting, stealing, and lying, doing whatever it takes for that next fix just to feel "normal." There is a saying in the substance abuse world. Drug addiction ends in death or imprisonment. There is a third option by the grace of God—a radical life change.

The second truth I learned that evening, and did not accept at first, was that prison may be part of the life change that is necessary. As I thought of my beautiful daughter, I could not square that. How could living in a dirty, stinking, overcrowded environment of debauchery and the worst kind of language and behavior be good?

In the genius of the Creator God, we are all different. Those experiencing substance abuse react differently for many reasons. One person may be on the wrong side of law enforcement for the first time, spend a night in the city jail, and be scared straight. Another might continue in their drug use until they are sent to a state prison for a time. Prison may be a time when they are forced to be clean because drugs may not be as available. (Most people I have talked to who have gone to men's or women's prisons say that drugs were just as available in prison as they were on the street.) Some fortunate folks may have a sensitive spirit and a strong enough will that the Spirit of God can reach their hearts and change them before they get into legal trouble or have their lives completely wrecked.

So we pray. And we hope. And we do everything within our power to keep them alive until they hit their bottom. There is another term that some use—hitting the wall. Amber puts it this way, that someone is not ready for help and healing until they are sick and tired of being sick and tired. One of our recovery guys was having a hard time and kept relapsing. I asked one of the veterans who had been clean for a few years how to deal with that. He said he was praying that so much trouble would come upon the relapsing addict that he would have to do something. I suppose that comes from someone who knows. At the height of his addiction, the recovery veteran was taking eight 80 mg OxyContins a day and was barely alive. Do you remember that they could cost up to $100 apiece? Hence, the crime and theft culture.

Today the trip to the bottom, or to the wall, is much more dangerous. King heroin, more and more the drug of choice due to its low cost, availability, and the addictive buzz it provides, is often laced with other chemicals to enhance the buzz or to dilute it so that the dealer can make it go farther. The user is never sure which one he is getting. So spin the Russian roulette bullet chamber and put the gun to your head. Let's load a little more and get a great buzz. Whoops—too late! This batch was strong. Unless someone close by has a dose of Narcan, a medicine to help reverse the effects of overdose, and the administrator has enough brain cells left to use it properly ... or maybe someone calls 911 and the emergency techs get there quickly enough with Narcan and other life-saving equipment and medicine ... or if neither happens, there will be another funeral service for someone who died too early. Another front page story in the hometown newspaper. As the senior pastor in Chapter 2 put it, the high cost of low living.

King David finally hit the wall. If we follow him through the Bible passages, he had a tough life. He finally was seated on the throne of Israel as he had been promised by Samuel the prophet. Along the way, II Samuel 5:13 tells us that David took more concubines and wives in Jerusalem, and more sons and daughters were born to him. He already had some beautiful women according to the scripture, but as the manner of kings were in that day, he got some more. Now, I don't pretend to understand the way that is supposed to work, but I do know that David crossed the line. While his warriors were out fighting, he saw one of their wives taking a bath on her rooftop. David didn't catch an accidental glance and turn away, knowing that would be the right thing to do. No, the lust that began with his eyes entered his heart and burst out onto his and Bathsheba's lives as full-blown sin and adultery. Then, as you probably remember, he had her husband Uriah murdered by having the Israel army abandon him on the front line of a hot battle. Talk about a lowlife. Now if you are reading this, have fought addiction, and are really down on yourself, just be reminded of this. As terrible as the sins are that you have committed, others have committed terrible sins as well. Jesus' blood and God's forgiveness covers them all even though we may still have to live with the earthly consequences of those sins.

David hit the wall. The prophet Nathan helped him. He told David a story (II Samuel 12) about a rich man who had plenty of livestock and a poor man who had just one little ewe sheep. The little sheep was raised like a member of the family. The poor man raised it, and it grew up with him and his children. It shared his food, drank from his cup, and even slept in his arms. It was like a daughter to him. The story continued in verses 4–6

(NIV) "Now a traveler came to the rich man, but the rich man refrained from taking one of his own sheep or cattle to prepare a meal for the traveler who had come to him. Instead, he took the ewe lamb that belonged to the poor man and prepared it for the one who had come to him. David burned with anger against the man and said to Nathan, "As surely as the Lord lives, the man who did this must die! He must pay for that lamb four times over, because he did such a thing and had no pity."

I can see the old prophet sticking his bony finger into the chest of King David when Nathan uttered those fateful words: "You are the man!" I imagine all color left David's face as he faced the awful truth. It may be like when the judge tells someone who has finally been caught for all the crimes against society caused by their addiction—it's payday! David fully confessed his sin and begged forgiveness, as recorded in Psalms 51:1, 2—"Have mercy on me, O God, according to your unfailing love, according to your great compassion blot out my transgressions. Wash away all my iniquity and cleanse me from my sin." And you know, there are some things God can't do—like not forgive confessed sin! Praise God! But David and Bathsheba paid a terrible price. Their precious little son died seven days after Nathan left the palace. That's how it works—forgiven sin but earthly consequences from what has already been put into motion.

In his infinite mercy God forgives the addict and anyone else of all they have committed when it is confessed to Him. But oh the results and fallout of that sin—what a horrible price. My wife and I cringed when we heard the judge sentence Amber to four years in a state prison, two years minimum with good behavior. We were the "model family"—Christians, active in our local church, and my wife and I had been teen leaders for twenty-five years. It just didn't make sense. Wait, what if the young man in the recovery meeting was right? What is prison wasn't the worst thing? What if prison is her bottom? At least she's alive!

CHAPTER **8**

An International Effort

G etting the $200,000 grant to clean out the asbestos in
the old school was a huge team effort. That was to be
the trademark of what had become known as the Field of Hope.
It is truly a community campus. Listen, this drug addiction culture is a community issue, and it will not be turned around
without the full support of the community. Thank you, Lord for
the support the Field of Hope has received. Letters of support
to obtain the grant were sent in by folks from law enforcement, the legal system, businesses, our state representative,
state senator, congressman, and even the townships where
the property resides. Wow! Looking back, it was quite a team
effort for sure! We had a celebration day when one of our
business partners printed us a banner sized check, and we
proudly displayed it in front of the Field of Hope—payable by
the USEPA to the Field of Hope. God blessed us with the main
building of the former high school including a full sized gym, a
former bus garage, a state-of-the-art sewage treatment plant,
forty-six acres of beautiful rolling land, a perfect football field,
and even a fishing pond.

The ministry had already started. One of our Vinton Baptist
Church folks started a car and truck repair shop, the Wheels
of Hope, in the former bus barn. Repairs were done for folks

in the community at a fair price and guaranteed work. Many folks were blessed to come to the shop and have their vehicles serviced. An added blessing was the twice-a-year free oil change and servicing event. Nobody was turned away. If folks let the garage boss know ahead of time so that he could order parts, they could get their vehicle serviced free of charge. Other repair suggestions besides the routine oil change, fluid checks, and an overall inspection were made if a person needed them. They might have them done later at the Wheels of Hope or somewhere else. That didn't matter—helping people who needed it did matter. I believe forty-five vehicles in one day was the record. The power lift helped in the effort, and at times there were three "NASCAR teams," as the garage boss affectionately called them, working at one time. All were volunteers, and all had a heart to help others.

Oh, on free service day, there was something else to offer the folks: a free breakfast and lunch if they happened to be there during those times. But more importantly, life change was offered. Wow, now there's a service for you! Often folks with other needs showed up: food, utilities that were about to be shut off, a sick loved one, and others. A circle of prayer was always followed by trying to meet the practical needs. Some folks gave their lives to Jesus and started attending church after experiencing the love of God at the Wheels of Hope.

I remember one beat up old SUV that had the brakes nearly fall off the wheels when it was lifted up on the hydraulic hoist. The garage boss said he couldn't let it go out like that, especially putting the gal who was driving it at risk. We discussed it because it needed all four brakes, rotors, and hydraulic cylinders. Let me interpret for those of you not familiar with the grease monkey jargon. That's a lot of cash—far more than the cost of a few quarts of oil and a filter. The parts alone were a few hundred dollars, even with the generous discount that our community partner parts supplier gave us. The parts supply house was owned by two dedicated Christian men. Enter the X Factor. When the supplier heard of our predicament, they donated some of the parts. The rest were paid by an impromptu offering collected from the workers. It is amazing what God will do when a group of people have a heart to do His work!

Another early outreach started at the Field of Hope was Integrity Archery. Another of the Vinton Baptist folks who was an avid bow hunter took note of the ideal habitat for deer and other wild game on the property. He also dressed up some hunting areas so that they could be accessed with a "side by side," a type of four wheeler that has four seats—two in the front and two rear seats. There are a couple of types of folks who would love to hunt but are not able to do that because of physical limitations: disabled veterans and other young people or adults with physical disabilities that prevent their walking through the woods or sneaking up on a deer for the thrill of a shot. Volunteers have manicured habitats to attract deer, built camouflaged deer "blinds" to hunt from, and recruited folks for the bow hunting trips. God has even provided a used side by side through the generous donations of supporters.

Some have been fortunate enough to bag a deer—to draw that bow string and see the arrow fly true to its target. Others have experienced the pure joy of flying through the fields, bouncing over a wooded path, or even splashing through a small stream in the four-wheeler. A special harness was added to the passenger's seat to help hold in those folks who are confined to a wheelchair and would have trouble staying upright without it! Hey, with that driver, I think I need harnessed up—it helps! Not saying he's a bad driver—he just likes to have fun. The neatest thing about all that driving, hunting, watching, and waiting is being immersed in the beautiful creation that our Creator God made for us to enjoy. It just doesn't get any better than that, especially for a person who thought they would never be able to enjoy the outdoors like that again. There's something about the beauty of God's creation. Cars, trucks, buildings, and other man-made things can be pretty special, but there is nothing in this world that compares to the beauty our Creator God prepared for us. Thank you, Jesus!

So the big day for the asbestos abatement project finally arrived. On December 10, 2012, the abatement contractor arrived. Yep, middle of December. It was sure to get cold before this project was finished as the winter temperatures in southern Ohio often dip into the negative numbers, and the snow usually flies. But these guys, and one gal, could really work. I knew something about asbestos work from my power plant experience, and I wondered how the crew would totally contain those large hallway spaces. When you remove asbestos, the entire work area has to be enclosed in plastic, and the atmosphere has to be under a slight vacuum so that no asbestos fibers can escape during the work. Never fear—three days later, the removal work began. This was an experienced crew who had worked in old schools and large buildings before—and it showed! We got to know the crew boss really well and then began to make friends with all the other workers.

The Wheels of Hope building was the only heated area on site. One of our talented VBC members had installed a propane furnace that he donated to the Field of Hope. Thank you, Jesus! The only other heat on the project was the temporary heaters in the makeshift staging area that the workers built. They made a large plastic room inside the gymnasium, and that served as the storage room for equipment and personal protective gear. With asbestos removal, no exposure is left to chance—full face respirators, plastic suits with total foot covering, gloves taped at the cuff, everything covered. So we set up the Wheels of Hope building as a break room and eating area since it had a fridge and microwave.

You know, working people have a few things in common. I'll put myself in that class. Although my hard physical work days may be behind me, I still don't know when to quit! Anyway, most of us like hot, black coffee. When you put the old forty-two-cup monster on early in the morning, good things are gonna happen. Now if you really want to win some hearts, and stomachs as well, serve up some famous Amish donuts. For the uninitiated, these things are huge. If you have a seven-inch Dixie dessert plate, you'll be lucky if said donut does not hang over the sides. Oh, and make no mistake. They are not lightly toasted in some triple-virgin olive oil. You can tell they are deep fried, maybe in good ole farm lard, and the sugar glaze ain't fake. I'll tell you one thing about Amish donuts. You had better be working hard if you eat one, because I don't think the box was big enough for the info sticker—calories, fat content, and warnings from all the appropriate medical professions. But the Amish folks work hard, and so did this crew!

Ah, the Southeast Ohio cuisine. One day we had the famous Italian foot longs from Gallipolis—the main town in Gallia County. Many years ago a fellow moved to our fair town from Italy, made his famous sauce, and his family has had a successful foot long business ever since. Now they say these footers stay with you all day long, if you know what I mean. Anyway, I thought I had bought too many and was wondering what to do with the left overs. Fresh hot dogs in the steamed buns really don't keep well. Well, I didn't have to worry about that. They all disappeared in near record time! On another occasion our Integrity Archery leader, who is also an excellent chef, prepared barbecue on his homemade wood cooker. It just doesn't get any better. Serve that up with some homemade ice cream, and I am not sure this crew really wanted to go back home.

Now home—that was an interesting place. The contractor pulled folks from the labor pool, and all of them made competitive wages. We know because we had to pass two federal audits, and besides, as followers of Jesus, we should be fair to our fellow men and women in all aspects of life! As we got to know the workers, we realized we had quite an international crew! They were from Mexico, Nicaragua, El Salvador, and oh yes, the good ole USA. It was really neat to get to know them and all their different cultures. The fellow from Nicaragua was the son of a pastor, and he was a really fine fellow. We talked to all of them about Jesus. The Field of Hope is a faith-based non-profit, and we are not ashamed of that. Quite the contrary, the Spirit of God is there, and we sense His work often. He worked in that group of folks, drawing us together, having no accidents, and finishing the job in great time despite some nasty winter weather. Now the Field of Hope had expanded its community to the world! What a blessing!

The work and cleanup was completed, samples were taken, and the lab results came back. The building was given a clean bill of health. All who had seen it in the early days of ownership realized what a remarkable and important milestone that was! It was all coming into focus. This tattered and junked up building was being cleaned up, raised to new life, and destined to serve a higher purpose. Just like the ones who would come. I know this sounds crazy, and please don't commit me. Sometimes as we walk the hallways we can hear the sounds of lives being rebuilt from the ravages of drug abuse and other abuse that sin has to offer. We can hear the laughter of children who once hid behind the couch, not knowing what would happen if they were found. We hear the sounds of the X Factor at work—bringing lives from the scrap heap of humanity to a new purpose, a higher purpose, a purpose that He had for them from their beginning in the womb. Psalm 139:13–16 (MSG) says "Oh yes, you shaped me first inside, then out, you formed me in my mother's womb. I thank you, High God—you're breathtaking! Body and soul, I am marvelously made! I worship in adoration—what a creation! You know me inside and out, you know every bone in my body. You know exactly how I was made, bit by bit, how I was sculpted from nothing into something. Like an open book, you watched me grow from conception to birth; all the stages of my life were spread out before you. The days of my life all prepared before I'd even lived one day."

May God take them from the scrap heap of fallen humanity and change them into the beautiful person He created them to be. Amen.

CHAPTER 9

That Ain't Normal

My wife and I sat in the courtroom, joined by one of my two sisters, our other two daughters, our pastor and his dear wife, and a close friend who was also living through the fire of an adult family member struggling with substance abuse. Our lawyer was a public defender. He was doing his best, and we supported him by doing all the work we could— my wife especially was very helpful. It is a familiar story to those who have experienced it—funds ravaged by trying to keep a loved one alive, supporting them and their child in our case, physically and emotionally spent from worry and making decisions you never thought you would have to make, the list goes on. Maybe the guy at the Recovery meeting was right. Maybe prison isn't the worst that could happen. We desperately wanted something to happen that would turn this beautiful young lady's life around. And while I'm thinking of it—that's another weird thing about substance abuse. Many of the young adults who pass through the Gallia Strong Tower recovery outreach are talented, good looking, and have great personalities. Drug abuse is no respecter of persons, and many times the best and brightest are caught up with other folks just like us in Satan's chemical dependence snare.

The judge spoke those awful words that our lawyer told us would probably come. You cannot be prepared for that moment. You pray, you hope, you trust, but nothing can truly prepare you for that moment. "For these crimes committed against the state, you are sentenced to four years in a state prison. I hope you can be rehabilitated and find a productive life when you get out." Those were not the exact words, but the intent of what he said is there. Those who have been there will recognize them I am sure. Then began a crazy roller coaster ride that would last for the next two years. It was a time of great trial, and yet God gave us some of the most precious blessings of our lives during that time. Amber was sent to Franklin Pre-Release on the south side of Columbus, Ohio. It was called a pre-release because most of the inmates were relatively short timers. Our lawyer told us that with good behavior Amber could hopefully get a judicial release in two years. That is normally how it works—if everything falls into place, the total sentence often does not have to be served. That is especially true for non-violent drug offenders.

There are some wonderful moments in life. When you see that new-born child for the first time, that special sunrise that colors the sky and meets the earth in a beautiful panorama of God's created colors, or meeting the one you love for life and realizing it for the first time. Wow! There are also some life moments that are so devastating that they shake us to the core, challenge who we are, and cause us to do some real soul searching. I am not sure how that happens if you do not have the Spirit of the Creator God in your life to walk with you. Try these on for size—seeing the one you have loved and nurtured for many years lying in a coffin after losing the battle with drug addiction, seeing a strong young person leave for a war you do not understand, and then seeing them return in a ceremonial coffin, or watching a person so full of life have their very being slowly drained out of them through drug abuse. Here is one you can't appreciate until you experience it—seeing the one you raised with so much promise and hope walking in an orange suit chained with handcuffs and leg irons.

A few of us men from the Recovery outreach visited a guy in a regional jail who had been in and out of prison for several years. He had determined to get it right this time. He was a great looking guy, and I told him he looked pretty good even in a jail outfit. You could tell he worked out even though locked up. His reply was classic—"I hate orange." Seeing our daughter in prison orange would not be our last unsettling "first" as we traveled this road with her and her daughter. You will not know the exact time the inmate is transported from the county jail to a state prison for security reasons. You have to pretty much find that out on your own.

When you enter this world of whether or how to support a loved one in prison, you really have to pour out your heart to God and ask Him to help you make some foundational choices in your life. How far do we go to keep a real relationship going between our daughter the mother and her young daughter, our granddaughter? Is a prison visitation environment really one we want our granddaughter to experience? Please understand dear reader, I'm not saying this is wrong or right for you. Everyone has to figure that out for themselves and within their ability to carry out a decision. We decided that the mother-daughter relationship was so important that we should visit every weekend. For two years we made the hundred-mile, 2-and-a-half-hour trip to Columbus each Saturday or Sunday. I think we missed two weekends during that time, one from dealing with the passing of one of our parents. Visiting started at 9 AM, so we would load into the vehicle about 6 AM, normally on Saturday morning. We would make a bed for our little five-year-old granddaughter, and she would fake staying asleep so I would carry her out of her bed and load her into the vehicle. There was a "mobile bed" with a pillow and one of her favorite blankets in the back seat. Normally our only stop was at the McDonald's in south Columbus for breakfast to go, and our granddaughter changed out of her PJs. We got to know the Saturday/Sunday morning crowd by name! The old fellows and gals looked forward to our coming, joked with us, and made over our granddaughter. We got to pray with them in some of their difficult life situations as well. What a hoot!

Learning the initial check-in and the procedure of a prison visit is really different—you have to be there. At times you feel like the one who is incarcerated, and you get a little taste of having your freedoms taken away. Prison workers are like every other group of workers—there are some good ones with a heart for their work and there are some who are only there for what they can get out of it for themselves. Those of you who have experienced life know exactly what I mean. The check-in process was tough at first. You had to be careful what you wore—certain clothing was not allowed, and any metal would set off the body scanner requiring you to step aside and lose valuable visiting time with an individual body scan. One of the guards, or CO's as they are known, would take you aside and use a detection wand to go over your whole body. You would have to adequately explain or remove any metal. Forget taking any pictures, books, papers of any kind, cell phone—you get the picture. You couldn't bring anything in with you except the bare necessities, like baby food if you had a little one. Oh, and take some cash for the over-priced vending machines if you wanted to celebrate the visit with some food and drink. Most of the inmates looked forward to that most normal meal of the week when they got a visit that included vending machine food. We got a kick out of watching some of the same folks get their favorites week after week.

Just let me say right here that we met some wonderful prison worker folks during this process that made the grumpy ones easier to take. You have to consider who they are dealing with as well—some prisoners lying and trying to manipulate them, visitors trying to bring contraband into the visiting room, and some just plain nasty people. When you live in that world for a while, you meet some interesting folks to say the least. The prison folks have to let them all in if they qualify with their ID and their presence on the visitor approval list. Just when you think you have it rough, try this one on for size. My wife and I were physically well for the travel and taking care of our young grandchild. We saw grandparents much older than us with multiple kids struggling to make it through the check-in line to see Mommy. Sometimes it was obvious that not all the kids had the same dad. And while many were closer to the prison than us, some were much farther away. Then we experienced the joy on our granddaughter's face when she saw her mommy. We heard her shrieks of joy when mommy balanced her on her feet as she lay with her back on the floor and then threw her up in the air as they wrestled on the floor. We knew that keeping that relationship alive was a great thing to do! Amber's daughter was so innocent. She prayed every night for her mommy. When people asked where her mom was, she told them: "She's in prison for now." It became the new normal for her fragile little life.

You were not supposed to talk to anyone except "your inmate" during the visiting time, but we did get to interact in the very small waiting room before going in. Some of the stories will tear your heart in two. You're not allowed to bring books into the visiting room, but they did have a book case full of them that you could read. Many were children's books, but we found several Bibles there as well. Thank you, Jesus. I would prepare a devotion to share with Amber each week when we visited because I wanted her to hear form the Word and give God a chance to work in her heart. Some of the honor inmates who worked in the visitors' room enjoyed the Bible study and prayer as well and would join us as best they could. I suppose somebody didn't like what we were doing, and maybe we technically stretched the rules by engaging someone other than our "our inmate." We were told to only talk to the person we came to visit or we would not be allowed to come to the visiting time.

We really enjoyed our little small group though, and I believed that some of them were growing in Christ. We always had a prayer time and included their requests. You would think Bible study would be encouraged, not discouraged in a state prison! Anyway, God gave me discernment about the situation. So the next Saturday we went to the visitation room, as we always did, and I visited the book case to get a Bible and read the passage God had given me for the day. We sat at the little table with four chairs. Amber had to always be facing the guard on duty. I announced with a louder than normal voice, "We are going to have devotions with Amber. If anyone wants to listen, I suppose you can." We had gotten a table near the workers who liked to join us. We shared the Word of God and prayed, and He blessed our time together.

I believe in our wonderful democratic system of government. I believe in and support our judicial and penal institutions as they struggle to protect our society. But I am reminded of how the apostles were put in prison for preaching the Word. An angel let them out, and then they started again. Acts 54:27–32 (NIV) picks up the account: "The apostles were brought in and made to appear before the Sanhedrin to be questioned by the high priest. "We gave you strict orders not to teach in this name," he said. "Yet you have filled Jerusalem with your teaching and are determined to make us guilty of this man's blood." Peter and the other apostles replied: "We must obey God rather than human beings! The God of our ancestors raised Jesus from the dead—whom you killed by hanging him on a cross. God exalted him to his own right hand as Prince and Savior that he might bring Israel to repentance and forgive their sins. We are witnesses of these things, and so is the Holy Spirit, whom God has given to those who obey him." Well, God blessed that precious time together—can I get a witness?

We became acquainted with the prison chaplain—a most gracious man with a tremendous heart for God. He was a black man from the city, and we were southeast Ohio hillbillies, but we soon formed a genuine bond cemented by our common faith in our Creator God. We began attending the monthly family nights where the chaplain would preach and the women would provide the music with their choir. Family members were allowed to join their imprisoned loved one. We really enjoyed the services. I wondered the first time we attended services how the preaching would go. I knew enough about what went on in the prison that I figured he would pull his Biblical punches when it came to moral living and same gender relationships.

Boy was I wrong! The chaplain probably got more Amens from our Amen corner than he had for a while—he preached a great message of repentance, salvation, and hope! We formed such a friendship. He told me later that he wondered, "who is this guy who brings his wife and granddaughter all that way every week to see their daughter?" I suppose that started the admiration we had for each other as we both served in this difficult place.

Our Gallia strong Tower recovery outreach had a rockin' praise band at the time and a number of folks with a powerful testimony about deliverance from the drug culture and a life of crime. I asked the chaplain if we could come and share in a family service one Sunday evening. At first he was resistant because an inmate's family was not supposed to have that role. We prayed about it, and the next time we saw the chaplain I told him that I wouldn't have a part of the service but that others would do that. I would just sit quietly by and enjoy the service. He reluctantly agreed. He told my daughter later, "That dad of yours is pretty persistent, isn't he?" He was being really nice to put it that way. You could say that a lot of different ways! So the day arrived. My wife and I and our granddaughter had done the morning visit, and now we were waiting at the prison entrance for the Gallia Strong Tower team to arrive for the evening service. The praise band came with all their equipment—drums, keyboard, guitars, and singers. The young pastor with a vision for the Field of Hope was there to preach. The Sanctify drama team was there to share the love and forgiveness of Jesus through drama. There were some ready to give their testimony, others there for the blessing and support. God was about to unleash something none of us expected.

The music ushered in the presence of God. We had a guitarist who was alleged to be one of the best in the state. He loved blues but could play contemporary Christian music straight from his soul. He also had a past. When the band cranked it up and the ladies started singing with our praise team, you could not hear a thing except the music and praise. It was so loud in that little room where about a hundred ladies squeezed in to be a part of the praise and worship that you could not hear what someone beside you was saying unless they shouted it. I remember our blessed leader of worship was red faced as she tried to lead the singing so that the others could follow. We would learn later that some had to be turned away from the services when they knew Vinton Baptist was coming because so many wanted to share the blessing. Nobody can predict when the Spirit of God will show up in power and strength, but my when He does, something good is going to happen. The testimony came from a young man who now directs the recovery outreach. OxyContin was his drug of choice, but he was addicted to many types of opiates during his dark days. God wonderfully saved him out of that experience to a life of loving Jesus and his young wife.

Then the pastor stood to preach. He drove a message straight from the Word of God to the heart of everyone there about God's love and forgiveness. He made sure that each one knew God's love was for them. It was invitation time, zero hour, the climax of the night. Was all of this just foo-foo dust to the women, or did it strike the heart? When the band played and the preacher prayed, they started coming. What an outpouring of decisions for Christ and to live a life dedicated to Him. What a flood of tears that can come only with the experience of genuine forgiveness that Jesus can uniquely give. The chaplain was crying too—wonderful tears of joy. We were joining him in the celebration. Then something unexpected, not normal, and totally shocking happened. Remember my promise not to be a part of the service and that being the deciding factor in us coming? The chaplain looked right at me through his tears and said, Brother Dennis—will you come and pray for us? As I made my way through that mass of praise team members and newfound sisters in Christ, I cannot explain the honor and joy that was mine just then. So much respect for the chaplain and so much respect for our God who poured this out on us. This was a special night—may God bless it forever, Amen!

Our friendship with the chaplain deepened, and we had another service. The Sanctify drama team had such a huge impact that the ladies' worship team at the prison started their own drama team. We were blessed to donate a CD player for their background music. But now God was really getting ready to show off. You are not going to believe what happened next. It was beyond anything we could have imagined. Ephesians 3:20–21 (MSG) puts it this way: "God can do anything, you know—far more than you could ever imagine or guess or request in your wildest dreams! He does it not by pushing us around but by working within us, his Spirit deeply and gently within us.

Glory to God in the church!
Glory to God in the Messiah, in Jesus!
Glory down all the generations!
Glory through all millennia! Oh, yes!"

CHAPTER **10**

He Covers It

S o God gave us this massive old high school building that
we truly believe He is going to use to help pull our community out of the despair of economic misery and the effects of the
drug abuse culture. I don't know if the cover picture gives you a
clear idea, but this school building is big. The gymnasium was
reputed to be the largest in the county in its day. The old North
Gallia High School also boasted some great basketball players.
That was the day of small county high schools, and some of
the cross-county rivalry games are still talked about! But now
only the ghosts of seasons past walked the gymnasium. The
wooden floor that the janitor kept immaculate and shiny was
covered in pigeon feathers, dead birds, and the waste from
their roosting in the roof supports at the top of the gym. It was
a royal mess! Note to the inexperienced: pigeon poop is nasty!
As one who worked with environmental and industrial hygiene
issues, I really felt that the bird waste was more of a potential
health hazard than the asbestos. Walking through that mess
and stirring up the dust was a lot more likely to happen than
disturbing the asbestos that was attached to the ceiling before
it was removed. What to do? Besides barricading that area
from traffic, we prayed as a team for wisdom, for sure.

Enter the X Factor. The Spirit of God guided our thoughts to the one place we knew had the equipment and trained personnel to properly handle this mess. The large utility I had worked for had several facilities in our area—power plants and service centers. The company has a community support arm that donates money, time, and material to support community projects. They like to partner with the community if possible. I knew that and had been on the utility side of that strategy on many occasions. The community relations folks really had a genuine heart to help out where they could and finances allowed. We found some great utility company folks to work with on the project—they were believers in Jesus and believers in the vision at the Field of Hope. There was only one truly safe way to get rid of all that mess—a vacuum truck with a filtered exhaust—a giant HEPA vacuum cleaner. They had one—at least a contractor who did a lot of work for them did. So we worked out a super agreement with the both of them—they would vacuum the waste and then disinfect the floor with a bleach solution. For the first time we saw light at the end of that nasty tunnel! When I held my breath and asked what the FOH part in the cost would be, a question was asked of me by the utility representative. "Why do you need a part?" That was an unbelievable blessing! Our budget is razor thin and faith-based—just like the outreach! Thank you, Jesus!

On the appointed day the workers and equipment came—what a great bunch of folks! The truck was fired up, and the workers suited up from head to toe, including respirators—this was the right way to do this nasty job! When the job was finished, the floor shined. Maybe it wouldn't pass the game night test from the former janitor, but it looked like a new floor to us! No more pigeon waste, and no more health hazard! Our granddaughter, who has always loved basketball, took the first shot on the "new" floor. The big glass backboards at each end of the gym were gone, but the four practice boards and rims were still there for cross court play. She was about six years old at the time. Naturally it hit the mark and banked in. Why should a grandpa expect anything less after a great experience like that? Hats off to my former company and to the wonderful folks who work for them and have a heart for the community! May God bless them. They were a part of the Psalm 9:18 (NIV) blessing "But God will never forget the needy."

But the gymnasium still had problems. The old rubber roof was about shot. One corner had lifted up and was beginning to peel off a large section if the wind caught it just right. I took some of the guys from our recovery outreach up on the roof. Armed with hammers, scrap wood, and a tool belt full of nails, we fastened the peeling roof section back down so it wouldn't lift up. We also saw the brittle condition of the rubber and realized that the fix was very temporary. This was all happening in the fall of the year, and we believed that the roof would not make it through another brutal southern Ohio winter. If the rubber roof failed, the whole support system that held it up was in danger. That would be hugely expensive to replace. Also more water would enter the gymnasium area and wreak havoc on the floor and walls with freezing and thawing—pooled water is just not a good idea in an unheated building! We had a great group of volunteer workers, but none of us were experienced enough to tackle a roof replacement job of this size!

So we got quotes on the work. The low bid from an experienced roofer came in at $62,300. It didn't matter what the bid was—raising the money would be a faith walk. Our meager account wouldn't support that at all. So we announced the need and began spreading the word, hoping and praying that potential supporters might catch the vision and help out. Well, bless God. We received a call that $50,000 would be donated to the project. So this is October, winter is coming, we have $50,000, and the contractor needs $12,300 more to complete the project. The contractor was a follower of Jesus, and his heart was in the FOH work. I called him and asked the question. "We have $50,000. Will you trust God with us for the rest by the end of the year and go ahead and do the work?"

As I held my breath for the reply, it was anticlimactic. "Let me call you back by tomorrow. I will have an answer then." Great. Do you like waiting as much as I do? Sometimes tomorrow can seem like such a long time. So—time to call our folks to prayer. And then the call from the contractor: "OK, we will do it." Thank you, Jesus. Now for another faith walk—where would the rest come from in the few short weeks before the end of the year?

We had planned a community meeting like the kind we held from time to time to keep our community supporters and anyone who wanted to become informed about progress, updating the vision, and generally keeping the work in front of folks. Good food and a fast moving program always helped. One of the FOH board members is an amateur chef on the side—he likes to cook for groups. You met him in the story about the asbestos workers. I call his famous barbecue "French Redneck Cuisine." It is always a hit at the community meetings. So by meeting time we had the $50,000 promised but lacked the remainder, and we needed something to tell the folks who were coming. I shared about the need. The contractor was at the meeting. I told the folks there was only one other person who wanted to see the need met even more than I did. He started laughing, and everyone knew who I was talking about. The Spirit of God was stirring. You could sense that another miracle was going to happen. I know that Philippians 4:19 (ASV) says "And my God shall supply every need of yours according to his riches in glory in Christ Jesus." But realizing the truth of that passage with a faith walk can be tough!

So the roof work started around the first of November, and the weather was ideal for the work—cool for working but warm enough that all the roof materials went together well. The old roof rubber was peeled off in sections and the new material put on the same day so that the roof-supporting panels were not exposed to any weather. The pastor challenged our church folks to help meet the need, and we were blessed that checks began coming in. There was not one large gift, but many smaller ones from folks who had caught the vision to bring healing to our little piece of southeastern Ohio. Community friends outside the church heard of the need and contributed as well. We will never be convinced that anyone but God was at this holy calculator. On December 31 the total that came in stood at $12,300. The FOH team and the Vinton Baptist congregation were thankful and blessed. The contractor was ecstatic. When, in our flesh, we don't know how the impossible will happen, He covers it!

CHAPTER 11

D Day

"Chap, we are reaching about a hundred or so at the family service nights. What do you think about an outside service? There's a natural flat spot that's raised out there in the yard where the praise band could set up and we could set the speakers. Maybe we could get all 500 women to hear the gospel." I was hoping the chaplain would be there for our Saturday visit, and sure enough, he came it to chat with us.

But then a real look of concern came over him. "Brother Dennis, that might be a great idea, but I know the state chaplain won't go for it. And you know, these women don't have to come. It has to be voluntary."

OK, it was my turn. I had such respect for the chaplain, but the Spirit of God was stirring the heart of the Strong Tower team about this. So where do we go from here? "Would you be willing to ask the state chaplain? Tell you what, we'll be praying all week for you and the state chaplain if you could just ask him."

"OK, I'll do it," he replied. "But I don't think he will go for it." We had another good visit at the Franklin Pre-Release. We had been in the visiting room enough and to several of the family services so that we had become friends with a number of the families who visited there. The ladies who were locked up enjoyed seeing us too. We weren't supposed to talk to them, but there is a special bond when you have worshipped together. You really don't have to say a lot.

The week went by like the others: fast and furious. There was the ever pressing work with the power company, ministry work at the church and with the Gallia Strong Tower recovery outreach, and trying to keep a semblance of balance with the rest of our family. We had two other daughters who were married and six other beautiful and talented grandkids to spread our love to besides Amber's daughter. Many days we prayed for grace, strength, wisdom, and discernment for us and our balancing act. We prayed that somehow Amber would be protected in prison and rekindle the love of Jesus that she once had. Amber's little curly headed girl prayed every night for her and for each of her cousins too. I have to believe that God has an ear for the little ones. He told the disciples to quit bustling them away and let them come to him. Matthew 19:13–15 (MSG) says "One day children were brought to Jesus in the hope that he would lay hands on them and pray over them. The disciples shooed them off. But Jesus intervened: "Let the children alone, don't prevent them from coming to me. God's kingdom is made up of people like these." After laying hands on them, he left." The faith of a child—when I get to talk to Jesus in glory, I'm going to ask Him about the power of a child's prayer. We do know the heart breaking reality that not all of them are answered the way we think they should be.

We also know that Isaiah 55:8–9 says we cannot know the mind of God (GW). "My thoughts are not your thoughts, and my ways are not your ways," declares the Lord. "Just as the heavens are higher than the earth, so my ways are higher than your ways, and my thoughts are higher than your thoughts." O God, however this turns out—we give it to You and thank you, for whatever You want to do in our lives. We thank you, for all the blessings You do give us. Our kids and grandkids are all healthy and strong—that is a blessing of God. Draw them all close to You we pray. Amen.

So the big day came. We packed up early to leave as always, and I carried our little traveler to the vehicle to lay her down in the makeshift bed for the next two hours. Next stop—McDonalds in south Columbus to eat, change clothes, and meet with the Saturday breakfast crew. The arrival and check-in at the visitors' center was uneventful as we knew the rules and all the folks who we would be interacting with by now. Here's a visitor tip—bring extra clothes for you and your kids. Some CO's may not like the open toed sandal/shoe selection, a shirt that is cut too low, and so on You will get the picture. Hey, they are people doing a job, and sometimes they have stuff going on at the job or at home that weighs on them. Just be prepared so you don't have to make an emergency run to the local super store and lose valuable visiting time. And be nice. That will be something different that the staff will remember. God bless you, Ma'am (and I mean it).

We were having a good visit. Amber and her daughter were coloring and making a little craft that the ladies over the play area had prepared. They really did a lot with a little to keep the little ones entertained. We would learn that some of them had little ones that they hadn't seen in years for one reason or another. Folks caught up in crime, and most of them involved substance abuse, burn their bridges with families, you see. They will take from their close family first to support their habit. We are not sure exactly why—ease of access, the belief that they won't be prosecuted because their family members love them, just not thinking of the long-term impact, and so on. Here's the deal. When a person is high and feels the strong physiological and psychological need to stay there, my saying is that the "chemical is driving the bus." We have to somehow separate the person from the addiction and love the person yet hate the destructive dependence on the chemicals. Sometimes we have to take a step back and get all that in its right place. Let's see, remember I John that was written to the Christian church? It clearly tells us that as Christians we will sin because the old human nature is still a part of us despite our becoming a new creation in Jesus.

I John 1:7–10 (NIV) says, "But if we walk in the light, as he is in the light, we have fellowship with one another, and the blood of Jesus, his Son, purifies us from all sin. If we claim to be without sin, we deceive ourselves and the truth is not in us. If we confess our sins, he is faithful and just and will forgive us our sins and purify us from all unrighteousness. If we claim we have not sinned, we make him out to be a liar and his word is not in us." My point is this. Do you really want to minister to those who have been caught up in addiction? They can see right through the window of your heart if you believe they have done something that you have not, and that you are better than them because of that particular sin you have not committed. Wow! You mean that I am no better than the ladies and men who wear the orange and bow to the command of the CO? Here's a better question for you. What sin did Jesus announce while hanging on the cross and turning into sin for us (II Corinthians 5:21) that He was not dying for? Please understand, I am not saying that law breakers should not face the consequences of their actions against society. The forgiving grace of God and obedience to the actions of an earthly justice system are both endorsed by the Word of God. I am sure that judges and juries across the country have lost sleep over walking the line between protecting society yet providing the grace to others that God has given to them. May God bless you in the struggle!

I saw the chaplain through the window walking past the administration offices. He was heading toward the visitation room. D-Day—the Decision that we believed would affect many lives. When the chaplain walked into the room, I knew the answer. His smile was so wide you could hardly see the rest of his face. "You don't have to tell me—I can see the answer," I said as I gave him a man hug. "I couldn't believe it," he said. The state chaplain didn't even hesitate. When I asked him about it, he said "Sure—sounds like a great idea." We both agreed—God's gonna do something special. The rest of the visit flew by, and I couldn't wait to get back and start sharing with the Strong Tower team. There were so many plans to make. We wanted this to be a day that nobody would ever forget—those sharing the Word in so many ways and the precious ladies who were locked up but would hear it.

Hope is a most powerful thing. We could spend the rest of this book sharing stories, but let a couple of them suffice for now. One precious lady had burned all her bridges. She had no family who was willing to take her in, and she was due to get out of prison in a few months. She had not seen her kids for over a year. She was able to earn a little money in prison, and she knew she would have some "mustering out" pay. So here's her future. She was being released to her home town—a city in Ohio. She had no means of getting there, so the prison folks were taking her. She would get out of the van with fifty dollars and a small bag of clothes. She knew the address of a homeless shelter and hoped they would have a bed open. That gal needed a huge shot of hope, and the One who knows the future is the only one who can give it to her. That is, unless she turns back to the life that incarcerated her in the first place. Returning inmates get hit hard in the court of public opinion, and sometimes the only way out they see is the old way. Give them a hand up. Most are not looking for a handout. Mr. or Ms. Businessperson, give them a shot. Church leaders, quit looking down your noses at them and love them like God called us to do. Jesus took the job as Judge, and He is the only one who can do it—leave that job to Him.

Another young gal told us she would keep in touch. Like a lot of them, we gave her our contact information and told her to call us when she got out. She was so blessed by her life changing experience of salvation through Christ at one of our services that she told us she was coming to our church to get baptized. They were not allowed to do baptisms in that prison. Well, what do you know? She got out and one day, to our surprise, we got a phone call. She wondered if she could come to our church to be baptized and whether her family could come to the service as well. We were overjoyed to do that, help them with gas to get to the church and back, even treating them to an after church meal. It's a good thing our church has a heart for the outcasts and broken. It was a real hoot when they walked through that door. We see lots of needy families through the food pantry and recovery outreaches, and this family fit the bill. Her dad asked if he could take pictures of the baptism, and we were glad to let him do that. We weren't quite ready though for his running back and forth across the stage in front of the baptistery waving a cell phone in the air! What a celebration! Hey, it was sweet. We sent them on their way full of joy from being in the presence of God and with a full tank of gas! Don't you think those may be the ones that Jesus would minister to?

"For I was hungry and you gave me nothing to eat, I was thirsty and you gave me nothing to drink, I was a stranger and you did not invite me in, I needed clothes and you did not clothe me, I was sick and in prison and you did not look after me.

"They also will answer, 'Lord, when did we see you hungry or thirsty or a stranger or needing clothes or sick or in prison, and did not help you?'

"He will reply, 'Truly I tell you, whatever you did not do for one of the least of these, you did not do for me.'

"Then they will go away to eternal punishment, but the righteous to eternal life" Matthew 25:44–46 (NIV).

The new D-Day was now September 13, 2009. It was a day that none of us who experienced it would ever forget. The X Factor showed up in power and strength!

CHAPTER 12

That'll Leave a Mark

O k, I don't want any of you nice readers to get mad at me. I am not going to bounce back over to the building construction right now, as amazing as that story is. Let's keep going with the event that would change our lives forever—all who witnessed it or had a part in it that day. There were so many details, and we longed for the Spirit of God to move in a mighty way and impact the lives of many. Our rockin' praise band was primed and ready. The Sanctify drama team had some powerful dramas prepared, the singers had sought the face of God about what to present. I had talked to Amber about how to reach the gals for Jesus—what could we share from the Word of God that would hit home with them? She encouraged me to keep it simple and understandable. Oh yes, the menu. We decided that good food always sets the tone for a great time of fellowship around the Word. The prison kitchen folks had decided to let us use the outside grill to cook, and they were going to provide drinks. So come join the party.

My wife and I and our granddaughter were the advance team. We had gone early for a visit and were waiting on the crew from Strong Tower and the other church folks in the parking lot. We knew who was supposed to come, but when you are working with volunteers, the proof is in the pudding—will they all show? The grillers arrived—a group of mission minded men from the church and Strong Tower who wanted to serve. Then the others showed—singers, the praise team with all their instruments, mics, cords, speakers, and other stuff, the Sanctify drama team, and those who came to counsel and had a heart for those caught up in substance abuse. They all had first-hand experience in the battlefield for the heart, soul, and body of those plagued with addiction. Just in case you are wondering why "those people chose" that lifestyle, Amber once told me after fighting twenty-one years of addiction, "Dad, nobody wants to be an addict." There you have it. They are trapped in the snare of the deceiver who promised to take away all the pain, anxiety, sleeplessness, heartache, and all the other stuff that goes with humanity. But as always with the Liar, paying the piper after dancing to the music carries a heavy credit card balance!

As anyone who has visited a state prison can attest, the check-in process can be a killer—the CO's need to make sure no contraband is hidden anywhere. And boy did we have some stuff to check in! I really wondered whether this thing would go even close to the proposed starting time. Enter the X Factor. One of our grillers had a real way with people. Now don't get me wrong—you know the kind of person who can make you feel at ease in about any circumstance. Well, he started working with the CO at the check-in desk, assuring her that everything was OK, helping look through all the cases, folders, and so on. She was a young black lady, beautiful in appearance and spirit. I don't suppose it hurt that he was calling her "brown sugar" by the time it was over. Well before long they were pushing stuff through in record time. It didn't hurt that the CO was a believer in Christ and saw very clearly what was about to happen. God has his agents everywhere! Something else happened that was really cool. The praise team drummer was a very talented high school kid who got lost in the music— you have seen those drummers. He loved to play. He showed up late with his ride, and the praise team was already tuning up. He said, "Man, they are warming up without me. I need to get in there!" What a heart to serve—anxious to get into a state prison. Thank you, Spirit of God for giving everyone that eagerness to serve and to allow Your entry into the hearts of the women through them.

And then there was Frank—a recovery legend. Frank was in his forties, had long hair, tattoos, and the look of the motorcycle gang member he had been—with the Mongols in northern California. He had been a part of the drug trade out there with Mexico until he realized his life wasn't worth much and was probably going to be cut short. He came east to live with gracious relatives and found his way by "happenstance" to our church. One day he was passing through the church parking lot driving a tractor to a hay field where he was supposed to work. The janitor was a perceptive guy and saw that Frank could benefit from the Gallia Strong Tower recovery outreach. Frank showed up by the grace of God and gave his life to Christ and His service. He has had some bumps in the road, but he is serving God today. Anyway, Frank was part of the griller team with a number of others, including (off duty) police officers, a coach, and our resident chef mentioned earlier. We were trying to figure out if Frank was there to help cook or pick up women. (That's a joke!) He had told me once that in his adult life he had spent more time in prison than out. Thank you, Jesus that he has spent no time in prison or jail since giving his heart to You.

So the grillers began fixing the 700 Bob Evans sausage sandwiches that we had brought to feed the 500 women inmates and all the CO's, administrators, or whoever else wanted to eat. We had cole slaw from Bob Evans as well, and heavenly desserts from the Park Front Diner, a local diner with an owner who specialized in outstanding baked goods, like German chocolate cupcakes! Sorry about that—if you're like me, your stomach is agreeing with the great food thing about now. The prison folks were going to fix baked potatoes and have drinks. We wanted this to be a time they would remember forever in every way. You know that Jesus often wrapped His ministry around good food—the last supper, fixing fish on the seashore after He raised from the dead, feeding the crowds—are a few times He did that. Just saying, there is something special about ministry and great food! So during the meal the music folks were setting up equipment and began warming up. The inmates ate and began gathering in the yard. They were sitting on the grass in front of the raised area that served as a speaking/music/drama stage. They kept coming and coming—when the service began, we estimated that all but about fifty of the 500 women were there. Several of the fifty were on the walking track, and they heard the message that went out.

Chap introduced me to the captain in charge of the facility for the day. She was a sharp, business-like lady who we liked instantly and felt very comfortable with. You knew she was in charge and had it all under control. When she began speaking, I could tell she was a believer in Christ. Certain words just flow out—you don't have to announce your faith when it shows like that. She hoped we would have a blessed service and offered to help in any way she could. When she gave us a hug, I knew it was on. You see, you are not supposed to touch anyone in prison. I am sure there are really good reasons for that. Embraces are to keep a distance between the two embracers so that you don't really touch. That's tough when you are ministering, and the Spirit of God tells you to confirm a decision with a heart-felt personal touch. The captain prayed with us and told the women in the counseling group where they could locate to receive any who would make a decision. The counselors were in a little circle close to the women in the crowd and below the ministry mound. We sensed the leading of the Spirit of God but were not prepared for what would happen.

The singing group had been singing and drawing the crowd in. That wasn't planned or on the agenda—it just happened by the leading of the Spirit of God. My privilege was to be the MC for the program and to bring the message from the Word. The praise band took a breather, and the mic and speaker system were working to perfection. God bless those behind the scenes who know how to do all that and are gifted enough to do in in just about any environment! Their reward will be great! I remember my first words like they were yesterday. "Ladies, we are sinners saved by grace—just like you. The only difference between us and you is that your sin got you sideways with the law and you ended up in here. By God's grace we are here too, to share the good news of freedom in Christ with you. If anyone senses a voice speaking to them about making a decision or praying with one of our counselors, don't wait—not for a song, invitation, prayer, or anything. Just get up and go. The counselors are there to pray with you and help in any way they can. Just get up and go." As soon as those words were out, they got up and went. It didn't stop for two hours. The counselors prayed, cried, and poured their hearts into the women who came. I was proud of Amber. Even though she was not where she needed to be yet, she took a number of women by the hand and led them to the prayer circle.

The service was amazing. The singers had songs that reached through the hardest of shells to touch the heart of the women—songs of redemption and love. The drama team did the *Everything* play about a young lady torn between a real Jesus and the world of alcohol and other substance abuse that ends in violence and possible suicide. One testimony was from a sheriff's deputy who had been hit in the back of the head by a falling tree while he was directing traffic during a snow storm. He should have died—the doctors said so. The prayers of brothers and sisters and God's Healing power proved otherwise. The docs were confounded. I will not stretch this to be sensational or to get a response from my dear readers. I do want to tell some amazing things the X Factor did that day. The praise band was jamming, and the music pushed right through you to reach your soul. I was standing up to enter the message time in the midst of that, and God spoke to me very plainly. I'm gonna tell you that doesn't happen often, but it did that day. He told me to hand the mic to the lead guitar player. Now this guy was extremely talented, and I love to hear him play. Like a lot of folks with a heart for the recovery outreach, he had a rough history. He was a little thin on top but had curly hair that bounced down each side of his head to ride on his neck and shoulders. I looked at him and asked, "Do you have something to say?" He wasn't on the program, and that wasn't supposed to happen. I was rolling the spiritual dice—listening to the X Factor because I had not heard our guitar player speak that much publicly and didn't know what might come out. He grabbed the mic like he was waiting on it.

He began, "The first thing I want to tell you ladies is that the shirt I have on is special." (It didn't look special to me—looked like a funky old tee shirt.) But he continued, "I know it's mine because my name is written inside the neck of it." The ladies erupted in a huge round of applause and support. You see, when you are in prison, you write your name on your clothes if you want the same ones back when they are washed. He continued with a great testimony of the grace and pardon of God even when your life spirals out of control. There is no testimony so effective with those in prison as the one from somebody who has been there and gotten victory. The power of God was on display, the X Factor had covered the prison yard. More ladies marched to the prayer circle. You know how us evangelicals are. We like to count—like notches on our spiritual guns. After over a hundred women made their ways to the prayer circle, I quit counting. OK God, I get it—You are getting it done—You get all the credit for eternity!!

The message started with the Fall—Satan's prideful fall from grace described so well in Isaiah 14:12–15, (GW) "How you have fallen from heaven, you morning star, son of the dawn! How you have been cut down to the ground, you conqueror of nations! You thought, "I'll go up to heaven and set up my throne above God's stars. I'll sit on the mountain far away in the north where the gods assemble. I'll go above the top of the clouds. I'll be like the Most High." Likely happening before the creation of Adam and Eve, they had an enemy and a third of heaven's angels who fell with him waiting on them. Genesis 2:6 says God breathed into the first man Adam the breath of life, then made Eve from a rib taken from Adam's side. Then they sinned when the fallen angel convinced them to disobey God by eating of the forbidden fruit. Curse you Adam and Eve, how could you do such a thing that passed your sinful nature down to all mankind? Yet Romans 3:23 (CEV) puts us all I the same boat. "All of us have sinned and fallen short of God's glory." So we would have done the same thing!

Is there a way to take care of this sin of all created men and women so that we can be with our Creator God some day? In the pre-Jesus days of the Bible Old Testament, animals were sacrificed for the sins of men. Through the prophet Moses God gave specific instructions about how that was to be done— through the priests, or leaders of their worship. Many, many animals died and their blood became the sacrifice for the sins of the people. The animal had to be perfect—without blemish. Then God sent the perfect sacrifice in the form of a man—the God-man Jesus. That most famous verse tells why God sent Him—John 3:16,17 (GNT) " For God loved the world so much that he gave his only Son, so that everyone who believes in him may not die but have eternal life." (GW) "God sent his Son into the world, not to condemn the world, but to save the world." Romans 5:8 (GNT) shows the extent of God's love and grace: "But God has shown us how much he loves us—it was while we were still sinners that Christ died for us!" Wow! He went first. He moved. Did you ever play chess or checkers? It's your move! Accept the gift. II Corinthians 5:21 (MOUNCE) says "He made him who knew no sin to be a sin-offering for us, so that in him we might become the righteousness of God." WOW— the final, perfect offering. Will you accept the Gift? Romans 8:1 (NLT) "So now there is no condemnation for those who belong to Christ Jesus." Leave condemnation. Enter grace and love. Forever. Jeremiah 29:11–13 (NIRV) says "I know the plans I have for you," announces the Lord. "I want you to enjoy success. I do not plan to harm you. I will give you hope for the years to come. Then you will call out to me. You will come and pray to me. And I will listen to you. When you look for me with all your heart, you will find me." Give up on your plan. Follow the Redeemer God's plan for your life. It gives you hope and a forever life with the One who loved you enough to take your sins on Himself and die for you.

Many did that day. We rednecks in southeast Ohio have a saying. When you are out working and someone takes a hit—maybe self-inflicted with a hand tool like a razor knife that cuts a hand, something falls and hits them and leaves a bump, maybe cutting firewood and a branch grazes them with a cut. As long as it isn't life threatening, you'll usually hear first and loudly, "That'll leave a mark!" Then a round of hearty agreement from all the fellow workers. God did that on the hearts of all who were there that day. We who were a part of it will never forget. It will never go away for eternity! He left a Mark.

CHAPTER 13

It's a Family Affair

Anyone who has experienced the pain of fighting substance abuse knows that it affects each family member who is connected to the one caught up in substance abuse. Listen to their stories:

Amber's Sister

I didn't understand why she just couldn't quit. I suppose understanding that would take a lot of study of the sickness. With kids of our own, working, and holding down a home, I just didn't have time to do that. I hated what she was putting my parents through. They had given her everything she needed to succeed, and she was just throwing it away.

And what about her daughter? She was just leaving her for mom and dad to take care of while she spent her day looking for the next high. I felt like my mom and dad needed to enjoy this time of their life when dad's work was winding down and he eventually took early retirement. I didn't want to see them worrying about what Amber was going to do next and also taking on the responsibility of raising another child.

I suppose the best word to describe my feelings was "anger." I loved my sister and wanted her to be better, but at the same time I was so angry about her actions. She was raised to know right from wrong, and she seemed to have no respect for authority or the law.

Amber's Sister #2

Amber and I were very close growing up and when we were younger, I was often referred to as her little mother. I had this constant need to take care of her (and others), encourage her, and love her. I loved both my sisters very much but had very different yet good relationships with them growing up. Thinking back to when I began to see a change in mine and our relationship with Amber was her rebellion at a very young age. As a teenager, she started missing curfews at home and getting caught in lies. I remember dad or mom going out at night to find her many times. Back then "drugs" were not talked about at home like they are today. When they finally found drugs for the first time, I remember how upset Amber and my parents were. It was the beginning of what would be a very long road.

Over time Amber became very good at lying, manipulating, and pursuing her own desires despite my parents discipline, taking things away, and trying to get her help. I remember that Amber was becoming this whole other person who no longer cared about us, her family, or herself. I do remember good times in between the bad as I began to make a life of my own with my husband and to build my own family. We had moments that still "seemed normal," but every family gathering began to show more of the toll that this terrible new lifestyle of addiction was taking. It seemed to be taking over not only Amber's life but the lives of my mother, father, and family as well.

When people say that the decisions you make in your life always affect someone else, that is very true! Even when you think you are only hurting yourself and it's your own life, that is not true. It's a lie, just like all the others you've heard from Satan: one time won't hurt, one drink, one hit, one pill. That "one" may start you down a road that you don't want to be on and that you may not be able to control.

As an adult I began to have a lot of anger toward the situation and the places it was pushing us to go. I saw a cycle of stealing, lying manipulation, sorrow, resentment, I'm sorry, then right back to lying again. I longed for freedom from that. Why do my parents have to deal with this daily? They should be enjoying their lives, going to events and parties for our families without interruptions or worries in their minds about when the next phone call will come or the next catastrophe happen. Having to keep things guarded all the time—medicine, money, valuables—just didn't seem fair. Despite all these problems, I was still loving my sister. I cannot tell you the heartfelt conversations we had and the letters I had written her, all with compassion but also anger, a lot of anger. I was on my knees and in the Word so much during that time looking for what God wanted me to say or not to say, do or not to do. I would try to tell Amber and my parents how I felt, but it seemed to go nowhere.

I got to a point of being done. I'm not proud of it. As Christians we *do not* give up. We love, we tolerate, we persevere—no matter what! All the things I was going through had begun to impact my life so deeply it affected my marriage and my new family I had been blessed with. I remember having conversations with my girls about things I didn't want to tell them about yet. Balancing it all was not easy. But God worked in a way I cannot explain. God gives us grace when we don't deserve it and strength when we don't have our own.

I continued praying and clinging to truths God had revealed to me. My other sister and I talked many times, encouraged each other, and we tried to do what we believed was right. Satan thought he was going to completely separate our families because of his work, but God had the last word. God always has the last word. Even though I got frustrated with Amber, I still loved her deeply and never doubted that God could restore her. I always cared for and loved my niece, Amber's daughter, who I felt was the one missing out on the most. She was so blessed to have my parents raising her. I am so glad she now has her mother to help her with all her birthday parties, taking her to ball games, and just loving and caring for her.

There are so many ups and downs, stories, opinions, emotions, and lessons learned when you go through something like this. If I did not have God first and the support of my family, I would not have made it through. When folks choose to abuse any substance, it is not just their choice. It involves everyone around them! I do believe that all sin is the same in God's eyes—some are just more visible than others. Life is tough, but with God *all* things are possible! When I didn't know what to do, or my parents didn't know, we looked to the only One who does, and He knew!

Amber's Mom

God gave me a wonderful husband and three beautiful daughters. We were living life, not everything perfect but a good life. We had a beautiful home, car to drive, Kevin had a good job, and we served faithfully in our local church. The girls were growing up, getting married, and having children. Amber was our baby, a freshman on the high school Blue Angels basketball team. One game she fell and came down wrong. When she hit the floor and couldn't get up, we knew right away it wasn't good news. She had ruptured her ACL and would face surgery—no more ball until rehabilitation was over. It was a long nine months, but she worked hard and came back, playing the next year with a special brace. But something was different. We began noticing some changes.

Our middle daughter shared a room with her and saw Amber picking at her skin with a pin. We didn't think a lot about that until other things began happening. She drew pictures of dark, evil-looking things. We thought it might be depression due to her ACL battle. We took her to a "Christian" counselor, and Amber convinced the counselor that the parents were the problem and she was good with the world. We monitored her activity as best we could and confronted her about smoking cigarettes, which she denied. She started driving and hanging out with friends—some we did not approve. She partied a lot and would come in late or tell us she was at a friend's house that she thought we would approve. We kind of knew and forbid her to hang with the wrong crowd, but you can't watch them 24/7. Her dad thought he smelled alcohol on her and smoke other than tobacco, and she got really mad when he confronted her.

But she made good grades and played basketball until she graduated. She turned down a basketball scholarship to study nursing at Rio Grande College. Then came the Myrtle Beach trip my husband told you about in Chapter 5. It was the week from Hell. She would disappear and come back drunk or high. The more pressure we applied, the more she pulled away. This was our first face-to-face encounter with the drug lifestyle, and we didn't know what to do. I ordered books, got online, and learned all I could. I became a very good detective and was up all hours of the night figuring out where she was and who she was with. It was no use. She was spiraling down a hole that kept getting darker and deeper. It seemed that nobody had any answers. When addiction is driving the bus, nobody wins.

She had a regular boyfriend in high school, and they wanted to get married when they graduated. We thought it might settle her down. They attended church and had a nice outdoor wedding on our front porch. Little did we know, the combination was not good. When Amber got pregnant, she stopped everything—even smoking. They rededicated their lives to the Lord, and things seemed pretty good for a couple of years. Relapse came with a vengeance. Amber was one quarter away from being an RN when she went out of control, was stealing to support her and her husband's habit, and landed in jail. Her daughter was about three years old, and we had her most of the time. She just got probation because of a first offense. She tried to stay under the radar, but her continued stealing put her in state prison for two years.

I was now a very co-dependent mother and grandmother, although I didn't know what that meant yet. We had a little one to raise as we went to court to get full custody and started down a new road. My heart broke for Amber and her daughter because they truly loved each other. The little one only knew her momma was gone, and we decided to keep her in her mother's life—they needed each other. The weekly trip, missing only two in two years, was hard physically and emotionally. I wrote her every week, and letters, cards, and drawings went back and forth to keep the relationship and encouragement going. Our little granddaughter loved going to pre-school! We made many friends with other inmates, some of the workers, and the chaplain. I believe the ministry God gave us there opened our hearts to helping others struggling with addiction. God showed up and many lives were changed through the presentation of the gospel!

Amber seemed confused about life when she came home. Prison had not helped her. The wrong people and wrong things began showing up again. She had gotten a divorce just before going to prison but now ran off without our knowledge and married again. She was soon sentenced to two more years in prison for probation violation and other crimes. Satan was at work in all this and trying to divide our greater family as well. The other girls had families of their own to take care of, and since we all live close together, our decisions affected them. After much prayer we decided to let Amber stay with us, basically on house arrest, until her indictment. As the wheels of justice turn slowly, that turned out to be eight months. Many folks thought we should let her sit in jail. We knew nothing good would come of that. We felt we were fighting for her life because she had overdosed just before her arrest and nearly died; she was unresponsive for fourteen hours. Only by God's grace and mercy was she alive. We were at the end of our rope and hanging on for life itself! I prayed non-stop for our family. Addicts burn bridges with their families, and sometimes family members feel the need to break away for a while.

I saw a glimmer of hope as Amber's heart was turning. Being drug free helps a lot. There are physiological changes in the brain with drug use, and healing begins when it stops. She was going to church with us, reading her Bible, and we started a small group in our home on Sunday nights. With her help it grew to a large group, often with over thirty folks attending for food, a Bible study, and fellowship around a ping pong tournament and the Wii dance! (What a hoot! Have you ever seen Baptists dance?) She met a guy with a similar background and experiences at Recovery, and they seemed to be good for each other. Eight months later, the day came. We wondered why it was so long but looking back realized God was in it. She would serve her second term of two years in prison, but she was different this time—clean, a relationship with God, and a different attitude.

Anyone with a loved one in addiction knows the heartache of a family broken by the addiction, and it was the darkest time of my life. We were "parents" and grandparents to a little girl and grandparents to six other wonderful grandkids. How do you balance that? Lots of prayer and seeking God's face. Amber was changing—we visited about once a month due to our granddaughter's school and basketball activities, her boyfriend visited some, and one of our kids even took their family to see her. God was healing our family. There was a crisis when Amber and her boyfriend broke up for a while— try a long range relationship with one party locked up—pretty tough! She immersed herself in the Word of God to get through it. Her prison cell became a counseling center for others, and when she got home her Recovery Bible was tattered and well worn. I am reminded that "a worn out and beat up Bible represents a life that isn't."

Stay tuned for the rest of the story.

CHAPTER 14

Hope Rises from the Ruins

W here do you start with a huge building—30,000 square feet of former high school? We knew it had to be covered, or the rain running through the old failed flat roof would continue to deteriorate the building. As we began removing it, we found seven layers of old roofing in places—a thick and nasty mess! The estimate to replace the roof with a new metal one was $350,000—might as well have been $350 million— funds the Field of Hope did not have. Enter the X factor. The Spirit of God stirred hearts and lives of those who were able to provide, and it happened—unsolicited, just by folks with a heart for God knowing the tremendous need in our area for substance abuse rehabilitation. A donation came in form an anonymous donor for $350,000. Other funds came in from area businesses and individuals who caught the vision. Funds were needed for roof removal, equipment rental, and so on. What a community response to a community problem! The truth of Proverbs 29:18 was being played out (BRG) "Where there is no vision, the people perish: but he that keepeth the law, happy is he." In Ohio since 2012, the leading cause of accidental death has not been vehicle accidents but drug overdose. Lord, give us a vision to keep people from perishing!

The bane of all construction decisions is the color. We decided on a deep red for the roof—covered by the blood! It is indeed beautiful—a metal roof with a fifty-year guarantee! The roof construction took a while to complete—a whole new system of trusses had to be installed first. We were blessed that the talented contractor was able to use a number of folks from the Recovery outreach to help with roof construction plus removing the old roof and cleanup. We now needed to seal up the building to keep the weather and critters out so that inside revitalization could begin. The threefold vision for the building was taking shape—a regional food pantry, a youth center, and substance abuse rehabilitation center with rooms for life skills and job skills training, counseling offices, and a workshop for training and a revenue stream. The food pantry at the church had maxed out storage room and was serving about eight thousand people each year. By expanding to the Field of Hope, bulk food could be stored not only for our pantry but for distribution to other area pantries. The gym would be the heart of the youth center.

Once again by the amazing grace of God funding was provided through a range of community partners and donors to install the outside windows and doors, dress up the outside entrance, and put gutters and downspouts on the new roof. The local Rotary club donated building material to start building out the food pantry rooms and paint the gym when the building was ready. The building looks amazing, and the entrance of stacked stone with crosses in the door and on each side say to come on in—you will be welcomed, blessed, and find help here.

Then a funny thing happened on the way to rehab. Our area of Ohio is in desperate need of rehabilitation centers, for women in particular. The state recognized that and also recognized the work going on at the FOH. Our wonderful community network includes many local church supporters, local businesses and community groups, folks in the alcohol and drug recovery services, our state and federal representatives, the courts and law enforcement folks, and the caring team at the state Faith-Based Initiatives office. Capital funding was made available from the state if we qualified to build our first

Recovery House for women. After much negotiation and filing of forms, building plans, and budgets, the FOH was awarded matching funds to build a sixteen-person Recovery House! Praise God! The vision was becoming a reality. God willing the first of six planned Recovery houses will be built in 2016 right behind the main former school building. The half million dollars in capital funding has to be matched, and we are trusting God to do what only He can do once again. Wow—it keeps growing!

Psalms 75:1(GNT) "We give thanks to you, O God, we give thanks to you! We proclaim how great you are and tell of the wonderful things you have done." We can honestly say that it has been a joy to work with many caring folks who have represented our local, state, and federal government groups along the way. A true public servant is a beautiful person. That is the way it should be—a great leader once said we needed a government of the people, by the people, and for the people. Thank you, Mr. Lincoln for reminding us of that and for the brave souls who put it into practice.

We never want to take for granted what God is doing, and the X Factor works in such amazing ways—we know that the Spirit of God is all over the Field of Hope. Part of the matching funds will be work in kind from volunteers who will help with the building. If you are reading this, live within an hour of the property, have a tool belt, and can more or less follow building instructions, we need you. God is truly providing in ways we never foresaw to get His work done and to heal a community. We have a local business that gives its employees a community day to work for a non-profit like the FOH. Wow, can they work! We have to line up lots of work because these folks really get it done! I suppose it doesn't hurt that the last time we served filets to the workers cooked up by our Cajun chef. Did I mention the homemade ice cream? Anyway, if you are going to do something do it right! Colossians 3:23 (GW) puts it this way: "Whatever you do, do it wholeheartedly as though you were working for your real master and not merely for humans." The southern Ohio red-neck version says, "Git 'er done for God."

Here's a problem. When sixteen women start flushing, you better have a plan. Not many folks can get excited about a sewage plant, but when this former environmental guy laid his eyes on the old plant at the former school, I knew we had something special. That plant was put in a few years before the school went out of business, and it was a state-of-the-art treatment system. The vandals had taken care of the wiring and most of the equipment, but the tanks and large sand filters were still there. All it would take is money to rebuild—whoops! Once again our God provided. Local contractors are working with the FOH team and a certified engineer who is volunteering his time to rebuild the plant and added a couple of upgrades to make it better. The cost has been donated by a caring community member!

Many folks have "caught the vision" of the Field of Hope by walking around the building, hiking through the rolling hills, or pausing to skip a rock across the pond. Do you remember Frank? He had a place of worship and prayer by the pond—his favorite place in the world because he talked to his Creator there. Wonder why this place is so special? It was left for dead—full of asbestos and overgrown with thorns and brambles, and it had a messed up roof that leaked and busted-out windows. But now it is full of life. The new and reborn is replacing the old and dead. God didn't see it for what it was but for what it could be—kind of how He sees us. I realize God was giving to Israel Jeremiah 29:11 (ERV) "I say this because I know the plans that I have for you." This message is from the Lord. "I have good plans for you. I don't plan to hurt you. I plan to give you hope and a good future." But we believers are part of His family through Christ. I think He wants that for us. The FOH represents that. As the new brickwork, stucco trim, beautiful windows and doors are added, the property becomes a new creation—just as Jesus promised us in II Corinthians 5:17 when we give our lives to Him. (AMP) "Therefore if anyone is in Christ [that is, grafted in, joined to Him by faith in Him as Savior], he is a new creature [reborn and renewed by the Holy Spirit]; the old things [the previous moral and spiritual condition] have passed away. Behold, new things have come [because spiritual awakening brings a new life]."

CHAPTER **15**

Don't Ask, Just Trust

W hy was Amber's life preserved while another's is not? Why was Job tormented? The Bible describes him as one of the most righteous people ever. In Job 31:1 he even describes how he avoided the bane of mankind—lust (CJB) "I made a covenant with my eyes not to let them lust after any girl." Today's estimates are that about 75 percent of American adults succumb to the temptation of pornography. Job was righteous in that sin of the flesh yet was terribly tormented body, mind, and soul. Why? God knows—not my job to know, only to trust and pray. We shared Isaiah 55 earlier—His ways are higher than ours.

We were camping with the pastor of VBC who led a building program to get us in the current large church facility (for our area) where lots of outreach can happen. He was the one with the original vision for the FOH. He was in a wheelchair and had been for over a year. He is so determined and has a great heart. When we set up the camper, he was crawling around on the ground driving stakes to hold the awning and ground mat in place. He would not be denied the joy of camping. It took our whole team—my wife and I and the pastor's wife—to push/pull him into the camper for the night. The next day my wife and I had to leave the campground and help place my dad into hospice care. He passed away two weeks later. Unbeknownst to us until that evening, God had healed our pastor in the middle of the night that first night of camping. God told him at about 3 AM, "Today is the day of your healing. It is for such a time as this." Coincidentally, I had been praying and unable to sleep with all that was going on and glanced at my watch before finally falling to sleep—3 AM. You can read about the miracle in our pastor's book "Wheelchair for Sale."

The next day he not only walked for the first time in over a year but walked all over that campground. Before we left a few days later, he, I, and another brother in Christ ran a race. His doctor told him that wasn't possible due to the atrophy from all that time not walking. Wow—talk about the grace of God. All bets are off when the X Factor enters the picture.

But my dad died. How do you square that? He was one of the greatest men I know. Just one example—I put the pieces together after he died. I kept telling him he was overpaying his income taxes. I finally figured out that this old WWII vet and dedicated family man knew it—he was donating to the country he loved. My pastor told me something that "left a mark"—"God gave your dad his healing just as He gave me mine." That made sense. Dad had lived his three score and ten plus sixteen years (a total of eighty-six, for you modern translation readers.) He was a child of the King and ready to go. Dad didn't have to suffer any more from the ravages of the prostate cancer that had spread to his bones. Dad was at peace with no more pain—the old soldier had fought the fight and won!

I was invited to visit a family who was losing a beautiful young girl. Her life had spiraled out of control, and now she was lying in a critical care unit with a stabilizing crown on her head—a result of a traumatic car accident. Her healing, too, would come in a way described by her "song":

A broken body in a hospital bed,
A medical crown steadies her head.
How did she get here? What went wrong?
She danced to an all too familiar song.
Caught in the web by the father of lies
Who promised escape from all that denies
A life full of happiness, freedom from pain,
Only to join the crushed and blood stained.
Their name is legion in prisons and graves
Lives too early defined as sad slaves.
But wait—what is that pure and blinding light?
The Son of God in the darkest of night,
Has come to her side to set her free,
The One who was crushed on that rough Roman tree.
He knows her pain—the hole in her heart
He would fill it with love, a brand new start
She invited Him in—peace flushed that sweet face,
Death and pain step aside, you've lost the race.
And from that moment on, sweet victory
He lives in her heart for eternity.

Only able to squint through her barely open eyes and only able to respond with a weak nod of her head, she acknowledged that she knew Jesus loved her and died for her, and she accepted His free gift of salvation—the ultimate healing. Why did her life end a few days later? I don't know! She got her healing. Maybe God saved her from further pain. He used her life and death to stir the family to do great things for others—I know that. A great missionary friend of mine responded to all the mysteries of life in a compact and Biblical way: "God knows."

Amber's Mom

As the two years went by we saw a family that was being healed and a young lady changed by the grace of God coming home. Thank you, Jesus. A few months later she was married to the young man who visited her in prison, and she began schooling for a four-year degree in Drug and Alcohol Addiction Counseling. Today Amber has a successful career as a Drug and Alcohol Addiction Case Worker at the FOH Counseling Center. She is working with a great team who have a heart for others, led by the pastor of the church who is also the President of the FOH Board of Directors. Those who see her say she has a unique ability to empathize and to speak to the hearts of those going through the hell of addiction. The lessons learned in the prison cell with that old tattered Bible and women desperately seeking peace were at least as valuable as the lessons learned at Ohio Christian University. Would any of us have chosen that path of learning in the school of extreme behavior? Nope, we didn't have the foresight of our Creator God. He takes a mess and makes something new and wonderful out of it when we let Him—yield to His will.

God has healed our broken family—the last place I thought Satan would be able to work, but he knows our weaknesses. I truly feel that prayer, faith, and love brought us through the trial. Addiction is a disease that often has a darker and longer path that you could imagine. God's healing grace will set us free—where there is life, there is hope: John 8:32 (NIV) says "Then you will know the truth. And the truth will set you free." That is one of my favorite verses to share with the folks in recovery. Nobody wants to be an addict, but if you have the addictive gene, you can get hooked into a lifelong battle. But there is hope and victory in Jesus. Your Creator is the key to saying sober and living a clean life. Don't give people in addiction a handout. Give them a hand up to see God's grace at work and share how it can transform them. Never give up as long as there is breath to fight—your miracle may be just around the next bend.

Satan is the author of fear. He takes the hard things of our lives and makes them look like mountains that cannot be conquered. That fear keeps us from doing the next right thing. I Timothy 1:7 (GNV) says "For God hath not given to us the Spirit of fear, but of power, and of love, and of a sound mind." Let us be reminded once again that the Scripture tells us over three hundred times to not be afraid! That must be important!

After years of wrestling with our daughter's addiction, I realized there was nothing much I could do but give her to God and trust Him—for life, death, and His best for her. That is a hard prayer because as a mother, I would give my life for any of my children. Step out in faith and pray constantly. Nothing is too far gone that God cannot step in and fix it!

CHAPTER 16

Amber's Song
The Long, Dark Road to Redemption

How do people become addicts? My story started when I was around eleven years old. I knew I was different from my sisters because I was a tom boy, loved guns (not Barbie dolls), and it seemed I was always into trouble. As a child I never knew how to deal with the guilt, and shame, of getting into trouble a lot, so I turned to cutting. It made me feel better to hurt myself for the things I had done and just suppress that anger toward myself. My parents never knew I was a cutter until many years later when my sister saw me doing it and told on me. That was my first taste of euphoria. At the age of thirteen I had tried marijuana a couple of times with friends, and started having sex, but no big deal, right? Well, I loved how it made me feel. Instead of cutting, I could smoke weed, and to get a boy to love me, I could have sex. That was the year that I tore my ACL playing basketball, the one thing I was so good at, and made my father proud (who I thought I was always disappointing with my bad behavior). They put me on Lortabs for pain, and man where they better than weed, or cutting. By the end of my freshman year I had been used by boys at school for sex, I couldn't play ball, and I was unsure where I belonged. By the end of my senior year I had done LSD, cocaine, valiums, pain pills, and grew weed. Drinking and smoking weed was pretty regular for me at this point. I became pregnant shortly after graduating, and knew I could not raise a child, so my boyfriend convinced me to have an abortion. That gave me a great reason to stay high.

I had a college scholarship to play ball, but I chose nursing school instead. This is when I started getting in deep. Over the next three years my ex-husband and I sold weed, cocaine, and tried whatever was on the market. When I was twenty, I was introduced to my best friend for years to come, OxyContin. Once the monster got ahold of me there was nothing I wouldn't do for it. By the time I was twenty-one, I was shooting at least 120 mg just to feel "normal." School was no longer a priority, so I quit and became a thief. When I was brought in for questioning over a stolen safe, I thought no way, I put that in a pond, and it should have sunk. Sure enough, that was it—I was facing B&E charges and safe-cracking. I decided jail was not for me and withdrew from drugs in my parent's basement for a week. I was put on probation through the courts. For those of you that don't know what withdrawal is, imagine having the flu times ten.

I managed to get clean and stay clean for over a year and had my daughter during that time. I thought God finally gave me someone that loved me as much as I loved them. It wasn't long though and I started hanging out with "old friends" again, and my dear old friend OxyContin was right there waiting on me. My marriage was very toxic so I got divorced thinking that would solve the issue. Well it solved some but not all. It was in 2005 I got divorced and went back to my old ways. It is a horrible feeling knowing if you don't go do illegal things for money that day, and get pills, you will be deathly sick for at least three days, and unable to function. So off to rehab I went, hoping to stay out of legal trouble. Trouble found me there, I had a RSP (Receiving Stolen Property) warrant on me that I was unaware of. They allowed me to finish rehab, and once home I started going to Gallia Strong Tower as well.

My life spiraled into addiction again, and I remember being at a grave yard with a car full of stolen stuff, doing pills all the way home, and my parents wanting me home. I remember pulling in the driveway and thought I took all the pills trying to avoid drug charges (until I saw the police report). Then I remember drinking coal, then waking up handcuffed to the hospital bed many hours later. I remember seeing my daughter's face first thing and thinking, what have I done. During the times I was using I was a terrible mother. When I would go out and do "dirt," I left my daughter at my parents' house, and she had to stay there a lot.

I can try to lie about it, but going to prison scared me to death. You have heard stories, and watched the movies, but nothing prepares you for being dropped off by the police to a huge prison where you know you can't leave. I went to Franklin Prelease shortly after getting out of admissions in Hale cottage. That was a very fitting name, since the person sleeping next to you could have just killed someone, there are hardly any curtains on the showers, the walls between the toilets were about four feet tall, the CO's were mean, and there were many fights. Franklin was like a college campus compared to Marysville, where I was sent to later in round two. I did not take it seriously, went to the hole twice for misbehaving, and put up with sexual advances from male officers (another reason for me to use). The worse part about prison is having to listen to your child cry for you over the phone knowing there is absolutely nothing you can do about it. I was so grateful to have my parents watch over her. They brought her to see me every week, and I don't know how I would have made it without them.

Not even a year after my release from prison, I am worse than ever—not shooting dope but doing about a thousand dollars a day in OxyContin's or however much money I had. This time something was different though because I was sick of the life. I had a whole diary full of how I was probably going to prison for life. I wanted to stop so bad, but it seemed jail was my only way out. You know you are in a hole when jail is your only way out. At this point in life, I was sick of life, I was no kind of mother, daughter, sister, and I finally knew I was going to die or go to jail. I was freed on October 12, 2010 when the manhunt for me ended at my parent's house. In my mind I was going to jail for a very long time, and wanted to see my daughter one last time.

I woke up from my high in jail sick as a dog. I puked, crapped, and shook for three days. I was so embarrassed when my parents came to see me, and I couldn't stop shaking—had to keep leaving the visit or I would crap my pants. Once the fog lifted, you would think I would be upset, but man was I ever so happy. All my crap was exposed on the front page of the paper, I no longer had to lie; it was like a burden lifted off my shoulders. Now I am out of jail awaiting trial again. But this time something was different. I wanted to live more than I wanted to get high. My parents, church, and Celebrate Recovery helped show me what a "new kind of normal" could be for me. Being sober was great, no worrying about the law, what I had to steal today, where I was going to get pills from—it was freedom. So after eight months of the "good life" with my daughter and parents, I had to do my time. Back to prison for another two years. Again I am so glad my parents had custody of my daughter at this point.

Arriving at Marysville this time, I knew what to expect, but man, that place had gotten even crazier than before, or had I changed? This time around, I was going to get it right. I stayed in my Word every morning on my bunk. I watched as those around me snorted pills, took Suboxone, shot heroin, and destroyed their lives even more. My last stop was Dayton prison this time, and that is where I truly got on my knees and surrendered it all to God, and He showed up for me. One day I was facing many obstacles in prison, I prayed out loud in my cell, and not even a half hour later the obstacle was removed from my dorm. *Wow!* That was my first major flower, as I call them, from God. He gives them to me all the time to make my day or week better anymore—you just have to look for them.

After coming home in 2013, I married my great husband whom I had been talking to for over a year. I got my bachelor degree in substance abuse counseling and am now working at the Field of Hope as a case manager. I have always wanted to help other addicts so that hopefully they don't have to go down the path I have gone. My family has been restored—I have a great relationship with my sisters as well as with my parents. I received custody back of my daughter in 2014. To be honest, that was the biggest blessing in my life. God does restore families. I also lead one of the women's groups at Celebrate Recovery, since I finally graduated it after eight years. Addiction sucks, but I honestly believe no one enjoys being an addict. God gave me freedom. He can give it to you as well, or your loved ones. My family's prayers are what I believe kept me alive during all this, so never give up hope! Do not give up the fight, love the addict, not the sin, pray, and be willing to seek God like we seek drugs, daily. Joshua 1:9 got me through many rough days: "I command you—be strong and courageous! Do not be afraid or discouraged. For the Lord your God is with you wherever you go." God is the one person who will always forgive us, love us, never let us down, and always be there.

CHAPTER 17

Your Song

D ear reader, maybe you are suffering from the guilt of drug addiction. Or, as a loved one, guilt from what you think is the poor handling of the whole mess. God has some great news for you. Do you remember how Amber's mom said God could fix it? He can. He says so in no uncertain terms. Romans 8:1 (LEB) says that because of God's grace "Consequently, there is now no condemnation for those who are in Christ Jesus." The Message puts it this way: "With the arrival of Jesus, the Messiah, that fateful dilemma is resolved. Those who enter into Christ's being-here-for-us no longer have to live under a continuous, low-lying black cloud. A new power is in operation. The Spirit of life in Christ, like a strong wind, has magnificently cleared the air, freeing you from a fated lifetime of brutal tyranny at the hands of sin and death." How do you like that?

Freedom
No Condemnation
Clear Air and a Clean Soul

Does it sound too good to be true? If you have never become a new creation in Christ, now is the time. Give yourself to Him.

He created you and has a plan for your life. It is infinitely better than the one you have. Free your soul to follow the X Factor, and enjoy the ride. It will last forever. I'm going to paraphrase the Romans Road to freedom in Christ—look up the verses in your favorite Bible if you want to be sure of them.

Romans 3:23: All mankind is in the same boat—we have sinned and fall short of the glory that belongs to God.

Romans 6:23: The ultimate penalty for our sin has to be eternal death, but God gave us a gift of eternal life.

Romans 5:8, II Corinthians 5:21: He loved us so much that even in our sin, He stretched out his arms and died for us. He became our sin and offered himself as the ultimate sacrifice. When we accept the gift of forgiveness, God looks through Jesus when He sees us and can't see our sin because Jesus took it.

Romans 10:9, 10, 17: We are saved from our sin by asking forgiveness with our mouths and believing in what God did for us in our hearts. Say it and believe it. Anybody can do it—and that includes you, my friend.

Remember the book of I John? Forgiveness and a redirected life are offered to believers who have turned aside as well. Remember King David? He was a royal mess. But God forgave him and restored the joy of his salvation.

Next Steps:

God works through His church, and you have a local church near you who will be glad to take you in and love you. Search for that place and ask God to direct your path. Then join the church army—the gates of hell will not prevail against it. Obey the Great Commission of Jesus—get baptized and join that local group of believers. Then find the gift(s) that He has given to each of us. Use them for Him. You will experience no greater joy this side of heaven. When we get to heaven, look me up and let me know what amazing things God did in your life. I will be the guy taking care of the sewage plant. Ha ha. Have a great life with Jesus!! Make up your song.

And most of all, if you think
This road is too hard—I cannot travel it.
This addiction is too strong—I cannot kick it.
This pain is too great—I cannot stand it.
This temptation is too much—I cannot resist it.
My family is wrecked—I cannot fix it.
This life sucks—I cannot live it.

Then you have come to the place where God wants you.
That is because you finally realize you cannot do it but

GOD CAN

Thanks

Someone ought to write a book. OK, I finally heard it. Do you remember the story about the guy lost at sea and prayed for help? He was expecting a blazing miracle. A helicopter came, and he waved him off—not realizing that God was answering his prayer in a powerful way. Sometimes we just don't hear well. I suppose that is why God gave us two ears and one mouth, trying to gently tell us which is more important.

God really has done some amazing things in our little neck of the woods. It cannot be planned. One of the great truths God taught me when I came to Vinton Baptist Church was to recognize the voice of God and obey immediately. That person who was put in your path or that opportunity that just "popped up"—that, my friend, was no accident. That was the X Factor at work doing what He does best—seeing if we will exercise our faith to reach for the stars. He owns them, you know.

Wow, where do you start? So many people—friends, loved ones, pastors, co-workers in the ministry, and fellow warriors in the trenches no matter how dirty. When you fight together and bleed together, no matter what else happens, you are brothers and sisters in the Greater Battle. If you noticed, not many names were mentioned. Our intent is to give God the glory and not get in the way. And there have been so many. I know if I named folks, someone would be left out. My friends, be blessed if you were a part of this work of God that continues yet today. The tally is kept in eternity, and heaven will get us together again and with those impacted by the work of the Spirit.

Thanks to my wife who had to spend time alone while God allowed me to write this. She has walked with us and shown great wisdom in walking this land mine field of drug addiction. I love you forever sweetheart. Thanks to my family who have put up with a grandpa who doesn't know how to retire. Thanks to my fellow soldiers in the battle—you know who you are, and you are not afraid. You are just as comfortable in the jail cell, prison visiting room, or with a detoxing drug addict as you are anywhere else. You have worked until you had nothing left. You have stayed late when everyone else went home. You have made that trip when no one else would.

Thank you, Vinton Baptist for showing me and my family grace when we needed it most. Thank you, for teaching me how to be sensitive to the voice of God. Thank you, First Baptist and Faith Baptist for grounding me in the Word. Thank you, Word of Life Clubs for teaching me the habit of a daily quiet time and hiding God's Word in my heart. Thank you, Gallia Strong Tower for being a bright light in the lives of many who wander in the darkness of substance abuse. Your reward is coming.

Thank you, area businesses, community groups, churches, and the anonymous donors—you know who you are. Your work is kingdom work. When you made that decision to give, you were a part of the greater work at the Field of Hope.

Thank you, Ohio prison system for allowing us to serve you.

Thank you, State folks who gave us a chance. Thank you, Brownfield folks—you have a great program.. Thank you, state representatives, governor, attorney general, and all the folks at the office of Faith-Based Initiatives. We are in it together, and we are in it to win it.

Thank you, FOH Board of Directors. You are a talented, gifted, motivated, inspirational bunch who go above and beyond the call of duty. You keep this project between the lines and provide the vision to push it forward. Thank you, special friend I call the Sheriff because when you come to town or to a project, things happen!

Thank you, to all those who listened when the Spirit of God called your name. When the X Factor enters the path of our life, He often stretches us to limits we didn't know we had. Thank you, for being obedient with your finances, time, gifts, reputation, humility, and love.

You are all living out Psalms 41:1 (MSG): "Dignify those who are down on their luck; you'll feel good—that's what God does. God looks after us all, makes us robust with life— Lucky to be in the land, we're free from enemy worries. Whenever we're sick and in bed, God becomes our nurse, nurses us back to health." May God bless you all forever.

Thank you, those who are being healed and those who are yet to be healed by the Spirit of God through this wonderful outreach known as the Field of Hope. May the experience described in Psalms 9:9, 10 (MSG) be yours: "God's a safe-house for the battered, a sanctuary during bad times. The moment you arrive, you relax; you're never sorry you knocked."

And most of all, thank you, Jesus.

Thank you, Jesus.
Thank you, Jesus!

CPSIA information can be obtained
at www.ICGtesting.com
Printed in the USA
FSOW04n0243010317
31373FS